THE WELKIN

BOOKS BY LUCY KIRKWOOD
PUBLISHED BY TCG

Chimerica and Other Plays

Also Includes:

it felt empty when the heart went at first but it is alright now
NSFW
small hours
Tinderbox

The Children

THE WELKIN

Lucy Kirkwood

THEATRE COMMUNICATIONS GROUP
NEW YORK
2021

The Welkin is published by Theatre Communications Group, Inc., 520 Eighth Avenue, 24th Floor, New York, NY 10018-4156

This volume is published in arrangement with Nick Hern Books Limited, The Glasshouse, 49a Goldhawk Road, London W12 8QP

This publication is made possible in part by the New York State Council on the Arts with the support of Governor Andrew Cuomo and the New York State Legislature.

TCG books are exclusively distributed to the book trade by Consortium Book Sales and Distribution.

A catalogue record for this book is available from the Library of Congress.

ISBN 978-1-55936-986-2 (paperback)

Cover image: Photograph of Ria Zmitrowicz. Designed by the National Theatre Graphic Design Studio.

First TCG Edition, February 2021

The Welkin was first performed in the Lyttelton auditorium of the National Theatre, London, on 22 January 2020 (previews from 15 January). The cast was as follows:

THE ACCUSED
SALLY POPPY   Ria Zmitrowicz

THE JURY OF MATRONS
HANNAH RUSTED   Natasha Cottriall
JUDITH BREWER   Jenny Galloway
CHARLOTTE CARY   Haydn Gwynne
MARY MIDDLETON   Zainab Hasan
PEG CARTER   Aysha Kala
HELEN LUDLOW   Wendy Kweh
EMMA JENKINS   Cecilia Noble
ELIZABETH LUKE   Maxine Peake
KITTY GIVENS   Dawn Sievewright
SARAH SMITH   June Watson
ANN LAVENDER   Hara Yannas
SARAH HOLLIS   Brigid Zengeni

AND
MR COOMBES   Philip McGinley
FREDERICK POPPY/   Laurence Ubong Williams
    THE JUSTICE/DR WILLIS
KATY LUKE/ALICE WAX   Emily Hather
                                                      Ayomide Mustafa
                                                      Shani Smethurst
LADY WAX   Aysha Kala

Other parts played by members of the company

UNDERSTUDIES

SALLY POPPY	Natasha Cottriall
JUDITH BREWER/SARAH SMITH/CHARLOTTE CARY/ LADY WAX	Jules Melvin
MARY MIDDLETON/SARAH HOLLIS/EMMA JENKINS	Daneka Etchells
KITTY GIVENS/PEG CARTER/ HANNAH RUSTED/ HELEN LUDLOW	Shaofan Wilson
ELIZABETH LUKE/ ANN LAVENDER	Rebecca Todd
FREDERICK POPPY/ MR COOMBES/THE JUSTICE/ DR WILLIS	Daniel Norford

Director	James Macdonald
Set and Costume Designer	Bunny Christie
Lighting Designer	Lee Curran
Sound Designer	Carolyn Downing
Movement	Imogen Knight
Fight Directors	Rachel Bown-Williams and Ruth Cooper-Brown of RC-Annie Ltd
Vocal Arranger and Rehearsal Music Director	Osnat Schmool
Company Voice Work	Simon Money
Dialect Coach	Michaela Kennen
Staff Director	Sara Joyce

'When beggars die there are no comets seen'

Julius Caesar, Act II, Scene II

THE WELKIN

8

NOTE ON PLAY

I prefer the Justice to be a disembodied voice but this might be
an additional cast member. If live or recorded there should be
a sense his voice could be that of God. It must come from above.

The play is set in March of 1759 on the border of Norfolk and
Suffolk, in England.

The matrons can be of any ethnic background, indeed it is
crucial the group reflects the present-day population of the place
the play is being performed in, not East Anglia in the 1750s.

KEY

A dash (–) indicates an abrupt interruption.

A forward slash (/) indicates an overlapping.

An asterisk (*) indicates two lines that begin simultaneously.

A comma on its own line (,) indicates a beat, a breath, a shift in
the direction of thought.

Words in square brackets are not spoken aloud.

*This text went to press before the end of rehearsals and so may
differ slightly from the play as performed.*

ACT ONE

1. HOUSEWORK

CHARLOTTE CARY *is polishing pewter*
EMMA JENKINS *is soaping her husband's collars*
HANNAH RUSTED *is carrying pails of water on a yoke*
HELEN LUDLOW *is mending a dress by candlelight*
ANN LAVENDER *is changing a screaming baby*
KITTY GIVENS *is scrubbing a floor with sand and brushes*
PEG CARTER *is sweeping the floor and ceiling with a besom*
JUDITH BREWER *is using a smoothing stone to force creases from linen*
SARAH HOLLIS *is beating a rug*
MARY MIDDLETON *is kneading bread as she rocks a crib with her foot*
SARAH SMITH *is plucking a pheasant*
ELIZABETH LUKE *is drying washing at a wringing post*

The baby cries, the brush scrapes, the water slops, flour rises, feathers fall, silver squeaks, the broom and the carpet send up clouds of dust.

2. THE NIGHT IN QUESTION

The middle of the night. A labourer's house. SALLY POPPY, *in the dark, and* FREDERICK POPPY *with a single candle.* SALLY *has been searching for something. We cannot see her properly yet.*

FRED. Home then.

SALLY. Thought you'd be sleeping.

FRED. Four months.

SALLY. I had ten shillings and a nice piece of lace in that tin, where's that gone?

FRED. Four months and not one word.

SALLY. Only four was it? Felt like more. Where's my money Fred?

FRED. I spent that.

SALLY. That's not yours, I put that by.

FRED. You put that by from bilking me on butter, where you been?

SALLY. That's got like a midden in here, don't you know where the broom lives?

FRED. Sally.

SALLY. Thought I'd been away years. Thought I'd walk in here to find it all different and you with a long grey beard but everything's just the same but dirtier.

FRED. Wife, / where have you

SALLY. Disappointing.

FRED. where the fuck have you been?

,

SALLY. I wanted to see the comet when it came.

FRED. Comet?

SALLY. It has been predicted by Mr Halley, / don't you read the newspaper?

FRED. [don't] talk to me of comets wife, November you left
    this house on the back of another man's / horse

SALLY. Right, no

FRED. no, do not deny it, you were seen, so do not give me
    fucking sludder about comets Sally, though I don't doubt you
    were gazing at stars, flat on your back in a / ditch

SALLY. May I

FRED. I am speaking

SALLY. Oh.

FRED. at church I had to make out you'd gone to mind a sick
    cousin in Stowmarket. A lie, I told, in the house of God.

SALLY. Going to church is like housework, people judge you
    by how well you do it, it makes your back ache, and after
    you have done it, it needs doing all over again a week later.

FRED. That's a dry bob. But you cannot wash a soul as easily
    as you wash a floor.

SALLY. You are right Fred. Washing a floor is much harder,
    particularly when you have a dog as we do. Where is Poppet?

FRED. Tied up, out back.

SALLY. Fed?

    He puts the candle down and takes his belt off.

    SALLY *picks up the candle and uses it to light three more.*

FRED. No, not fed. She's lucky I have not broke her neck,
    feeding's too good for her, lift your skirts. Put your hands on
    the wall.

SALLY. Pick one. I can't do both.

    *She turns. We see her illuminated for the first time. Covered
    head to toe in blood.*

FRED. my God.

    He drops his belt.

    Are you hurt?

FRED *begins a frantic but tender examination, trying to locate the source of bleeding.*

Who has done this? Who has harmed you?

SALLY. No one has harmed me.

FRED. I cannot find a wound... where is / the?

SALLY. There is no wound. It is not my blood.

FRED. But... how / then

SALLY. You stink, by the way.

FRED. I... I have been shovelling out the earth closet...

SALLY. This parish is full of secrets and yet we spread our shit on the fields for all to see and eat the grain that grows in it.

FRED. Whose blood is it? Whose – my god – my god Sal, what was it, an accident?

SALLY *takes a hammer out of her pocket.*

SALLY. It was not an accident.

FRED. Whose blood is it? Sally whose blood? Speak maw!

SALLY. I'm having a baby. It ent yours.

He slaps her.

FRED. You liar

SALLY. I want my ten shillings. I need / to go away

FRED. you old drab

SALLY. and I must have something to pay the Midnight Woman when / the time comes

FRED. dirty, wicked bunter

SALLY. having a baby isn't / dirty

FRED. hedge-whore

SALLY. or maybe it is, it probably depends on who puts it in and who takes it out again – no.

He has grabbed the hammer, she shoves him away with force.

No. No more of that.

FRED *falls to his knees and looks up to Heaven.*

FRED. May God forgive you.

SALLY *yawns.*

SALLY. ['Scuse me] God isn't up there, Fred. He's inside us. In our bodies. In your body and mine and Poppet's too. He is in your blood and your flesh and your brain, which by the way looks like a dirty sponge that's been used to clean windows. A filthy grey thing. I'll say it one more time. I want my ten shillings. You can keep the lace.

FRED *sobs, fearful and wretched.*

FRED. What's happened gal? What you done?

From her other pocket SALLY *takes a long golden plait tied with a sky-blue ribbon. She uses one of the candles to set fire to it.*

Sally Poppy, you tell me right now where the Hell you've been!

SALLY. I've been to look at God.

Sudden black. In the dark the hard and continuous banging of a butter churn.

3. EXECUTION DAY

It is wash day, there are linens hung.
ELIZABETH LUKE *is churning butter.*
COOMBES *enters. A bunch of daffodils. One arm in a sling.*

COOMBES. Good day Mrs Luke.

ELIZABETH. Afternoon, Mr Coombes.

He watches her. She is conscious of his eyes on her.

You'll forgive me, I cannot stop to talk, this butter will not come.

He continues to watch her. Quietly:

Not now, Billy.

COOMBES. You did not come Thursday / last

ELIZABETH. Shhh.

COOMBES. I waited for you for an hour and a quarter.

ELIZABETH. I have told you I am done with it.

COOMBES. I cannot stop thinking about your commodity.

She sighs. Shifts her grip on the churn. Wipes sweat from her brow.

Where is the wrong in it? We are both widowed.

ELIZABETH. I am widowed Billy, your wife is very much alive.

COOMBES. Yes but she is gone to Lowestoft.

ELIZABETH. What do you want?

He offers the daffodils with a smile.

Billy!

COOMBES. Oh, alright. I come from the assizes. The Justice calls for a jury of matrons.

ELIZABETH. Does he want me?

COOMBES. He does.

ELIZABETH. Could he not have someone else?

COOMBES. I am sent to fetch you.

ELIZABETH. By name?

COOMBES. On account of your experience as midwife.

ELIZABETH. Could you tell him it is my Grand Wash today?

COOMBES. Justice cannot stop for your linens.

ELIZABETH. But could it not wait a little?

COOMBES. It is your civic duty.

ELIZABETH. It is an inconvenience.

COOMBES. What strong arms you have.

ELIZABETH. Billy.

COOMBES. They have caught and tried the murderers of little
Alice Wax.

She looks up, surprised. Pause.

ELIZABETH. I did not realise they had found the, that they had
found a body.

COOMBES. Two nights ago the curate noticed a preponderance
of crows above the old Pearl house. They found her in pieces
in two sacks stuffed up the fireplace.

ELIZABETH. Expect that is the closest a Wax child ever got to
sweeping a chimney.

COOMBES. Lizzy! A girl has been killed. And the Waxes are
a good family.

ELIZABETH. Certainly. They've a house full of decencies to
put between themselves and the rest of the world but now the
world has got in nonetheless.

COOMBES. What is the matter with you, they are in grief!

ELIZABETH. I'm sorry, I am tired.

COOMBES. It is only midday.

ELIZABETH. And yet I am tired Billy what is your question?

COOMBES. Lizzy / don't

ELIZABETH. I am sorry for Lady Wax, but seems to me people round here are too ready to mourn little girls and too slow to mourn grown men.

ELIZABETH *resumes churning*.

COOMBES. Look, you know I am sympathetic to your grievances, but John Wax is a gentleman –

ELIZABETH. John Wax has enclosed my sister's husband's pasture and given him instead a scrubby spit of land a quarter of the size, I would not dry my linens on it. And David Swain is hanged under the Black Act for killing two deer that were destroying his clover after many requests to John Wax that he should control his beasts.

COOMBES. He was apprised of the law.

ELIZABETH. He is hanged Billy! Hanged for old venison! There are evils happening in this country at present that are worse than the death of a child.

COOMBES. What of poor Lady Wax then? Her life will be an open wound.

ELIZABETH. Good. That's a woman who never had nothing taken from her in her whole life, perhaps the experience will sweeten her, like frost on a parsnip.

COOMBES. I never heard you speak so cruel before.

ELIZABETH. Well you never met me in the middle of my housework before.

She steps away from the churn, exhausted.

COOMBES. Give us a kiss.

ELIZABETH. No.

COOMBES. Go on.

She sighs. Checks they are not observed. She gives him a kiss. He strokes her head.

I ent gonna higgle with you Lizzy. But you ent being fair. The Waxes been decent to me.

ELIZABETH. Since when?

COOMBES. Since them's offered me work.

ELIZABETH. Doing what?

COOMBES. Scaring rooks.

ELIZABETH. That's child's work.

COOMBES. It's work.

ELIZABETH. Anyway, you ent a labourer. You're a thatcher.

COOMBES. Not with one arm I ent. That's been a hard old year that has, Lizzy.

ELIZABETH. I know.

COOMBES. I know you know, whole town knows, whole town laughs except the Waxes. A tied cottage they offered me this morning. A tied cottage, in my condition, I call that very Christian.

ELIZABETH. Which one?

COOMBES. You know where old Weasel Humphrey live?

ELIZABETH. That one that's always full of bees?

COOMBES. That's it. Spacious that is.

ELIZABETH *takes up the churn and continues to work.*

ELIZABETH. No, but I do feel wretched for Lady Wax. The child's bonnet was always goffered beautiful. And if there are murderers in our midst I am glad they are not at liberty.

COOMBES. They were apprehended last night. A man and a woman. Only took eighteen minutes to find them both guilty.

ELIZABETH. Not local people?

COOMBES. Thomas McKay was a stranger, come down from Scotland. He was hanged already this morning. You should have seen the crowds.

ELIZABETH. I do not care to watch the life going out of a body, I never have. And I have been locked in a dark room these past two days delivering Mrs Lovell of twins.

COOMBES. I heard only a son.

ELIZABETH. I delivered a girl as well.

COOMBES. Oh. And did / she?

ELIZABETH. no she lived only a few minutes.

COOMBES. Another? I am sorry for it darl.

He reaches for her gently. She lets herself be comforted.
A tenderness between them.

ELIZABETH. Mrs Lovell would not drink her caudle. And their
house is so cold, that was impossible to stop up all the
draughts.

COOMBES. Nobody blames you.

ELIZABETH *starts churning vigorously again.*

ELIZABETH. Twelve babies lost in as many months

COOMBES. It is / God's will.

ELIZABETH. and I am the very first person they blame, God?
No, they don't blame God. Nobody blames God when there
is a woman can be blamed instead. Who is the accomplice?
A foreigner too?

COOMBES. No, it is Sally Poppy, from Metfield.

ELIZABETH. Don't know her.

COOMBES. Fred Poppy's wife. Francis Cobb's daughter.

ELIZABETH *stops churning.*

ELIZABETH. Sally? Janet Cobb's girl?

COOMBES. Might have been predicted, the whole family is
hell-born, the father is a shit sack, the brother is no better, the
mother is a slamkin and all of them stub-faced and rank.
Sally is the same, been joining giblets with sailors since she
was ten years old.

ELIZABETH. Billy –

COOMBES. oh don't Billy me, you know that's true.

ELIZABETH. But... had she met the Wax child before?

COOMBES. Sally was employed as laundry mistress in the Wax house for a time.

ELIZABETH. Oh. I did not, and then did she quarrel with the girl?

COOMBES. No, by all accounts the girl doted on her and was distraught when she was dismissed.

ELIZABETH. Why was she dismissed?

COOMBES. Some stomachers disappeared from Lady Wax's wardrobe.

ELIZABETH. So, so, so Sally has confessed?

COOMBES. No, but she is guilty without question. Her husband says she arrived home in the middle of the night covered in blood with a hammer in her hand and laughed and laughed and rapped out a volley of oaths to the Devil.

ELIZABETH. I heard she was not very happy in her marriage.

COOMBES. Yes, at least the poor man is free now. A discontented wife is a Hell on earth.

ELIZABETH. And Sally is, she is sentenced to hang is she?

COOMBES. She is and she will, there's a crowd fifty-deep outside the assizes waiting to see it, but she pleads the belly. We have eleven women empanelled but must have a twelfth.

ELIZABETH *shakes her head, disturbed, and starts churning again.*

ELIZABETH. Find someone else, I cannot.

COOMBES. The girl is lying.

ELIZABETH. I cannot be the one to say so.

COOMBES. Alice's mother lies abed, dying of grief!

ELIZABETH. And what of Sally's mother?

COOMBES. What of her? Janet Cobb's loins have brought forth only terror.

ELIZABETH. She suffers too.

COOMBES. She has brought a devil into the world.

ELIZABETH. With respect, was I who brought Sally into the world. Janet merely contributed the screaming.

,

COOMBES. You delivered the girl?

ELIZABETH. Yes, she was my first.

COOMBES. Really? You must have / been

ELIZABETH. I was three days short of fourteen, my mother could not leave her bed, so I caught her instead and put her in Janet's arms.

She stops churning. Pause.

Dear little old girl.

COOMBES. Not any more she ain't. Biddy has a hang-gallows look if ever I saw one. Born on Newgate step, she was.

ELIZABETH. That's true there's creases in her character, but I do not believe she's a murderer.

COOMBES. You are in a minority. Trust me, there was soil on the mangle when that one was put through.

She goes on churning again.

ELIZABETH. Well. Perhaps motherhood will improve her.

COOMBES. There is no child Lizzy! It is pure gammon.

ELIZABETH. I believe her.

COOMBES. You have not even seen her!

ELIZABETH. I know she has been tried in a cold room by cold men on the word of a cold husband, with no one to speak for her and a mob outside the window. Even if she is lying I do not blame her, I would lie too. When a woman is being buried alive she will reach for even the grubbiest tool to dig herself out again.

COOMBES *moves behind her, puts a hand up her skirt, investigates.*

COOMBES. You would not talk this way if you spent but a minute with her. All the time I been bailiff, I have never encountered such wickedness, that is unthinkable there should be so much evil so close to home. She asked for a cup of water this morning. I found myself outside myself thinking: I am watching a devil drink a cup of water. How could the Devil deal in such dull things as cups of water?

He kisses her neck.

ELIZABETH. Perhaps she is not a devil. Perhaps she only lost her head in loyalty to one and now faces a hanging for it.

She stops churning. Deeply troubled. Removes COOMBES's *hand.*

COOMBES. Ah, now, what's this then? Cheer up doll. Go on, that is awful to me, to see you so miserable.

ELIZABETH. Please Billy. Tell the Justice I was not at home.

He sighs.

COOMBES. Oh, suit yourself. I'll not carry you there. We'll sit with eleven, go quicker without you, there ent a woman on that jury wants to see her live.

She looks up at him.

I hate it when we quarrel.

Pause.

ELIZABETH. Katy!

KATY *comes running on. She has been painted with brimstone and is bright yellow.*

COOMBES. Just the maid I was looking for.

He holds out the daffodils to KATY, *she takes them, pleased and shy.*

ELIZABETH. I must go with Mr Coombes. Fetch my shawl.

COOMBES. That's the job!

KATY *runs off again.*

ELIZABETH. And a loaf of bread!

ELIZABETH *moves quickly, collecting butter paddles, taking washing from the line.*

COOMBES. I thought she was better.

ELIZABETH. So did I. I clean and wash and clean and wash and still my children itch.

KATY *returns with* ELIZABETH*'s shawl and a loaf of bread.*

Take the churn. Here are the paddles for when the butter comes, and after, rinse the heavy linens. I'll be back to help you fold.

ELIZABETH *puts her shawl on and gathers the paddles.* KATY *starts churning. She watches the sky as she does.*

COOMBES. When's this old comet coming then Kit? You spend so much time searching that sky, reckon your neck's gonna get stuck like that.

KATY. Mr Halley said it shoulda come before Old Year's Night.

COOMBES. That's three months late then. I call that very rude.

KATY. I dassent miss it. I'll be dead before that comes round again.

COOMBES. You don't know that. That's in the future that is, you might live to a hundred, my granny did.

KATY. When does the future start?

COOMBES. Well. When the past ends, probly.

KATY. When does the past end?

COOMBES. Oh I dunno, reckon… reckon round about, uh… NOW!

He leaps on her, tickles her, she giggles.

ELIZABETH. I'd walk ahead if I were you Mr Coombes. That's stingy old weather, I won't dawdle, and your legs are shorter than mine.

He is hurt. She picks up the bread.

COOMBES. Leave that. Justice won't allow wittles.

COOMBES *exits.* ELIZABETH *hides the bread under her skirts.*

KATY. Where are you going?

ELIZABETH. To the assizes. There is a woman there in need of help. She is a nasty, stupid, wicked wretch, and I mean to save her life.

She exits. KATY *keeps churning the butter.*
We watch for as long as feels slightly too long.
It is boring, hard work and it makes her arms ache.
Then, black.

4. THE EMPANELLING

The sound of the butter churn continues. In the dark we hear the JUSTICE's *voice.*

JUSTICE. Come forward, Mrs Charlotte Cary.

CHARLOTTE CARY *comes forward out of the dark and into light.*

Lay your right hand upon the Book, look upon the prisoner and harken to your oath: you, as fore-matron to this jury, swear that you will diligently enquire, search and try, whether Sally Poppy, now prisoner at the bar, be with quick child or not, and thereof give a true verdict, according to the bed of your skill and knowledge. So help you God. Kiss the Book.

CHARLOTTE. Mrs Charlotte Cary, widow of Colonel Samuel Cary. I am a visitor to this parish from Colchester. Two daughters, both grown. My hopes for a walk were dashed by a turned ankle so I thought to entertain myself at the trial. I have a dinner engagement at five. I have been promised boiled bacon. I have a special fondness for boiled bacon.

CHARLOTTE *kisses the book and goes back into the dark.*

JUSTICE. Come forward, Mrs Hannah Rusted.

The next matron comes out of the dark, HANNAH RUSTED.

Lay your right hand upon the Book. The same oath / which your fore-matron has taken on her part, you shall well and truly observe and keep on your own respective part. So help you God. Kiss the book.

HANNAH. I am Hannah Rusted. My husband's wages have gone down as the price of bread rises. We have three children and for the most part we rub along well enough but since Christmas I have been dreaming dreams wherein my husband is press-ganged into the Navy and when I wake up I am so happy.

HANNAH *kisses the book and goes back into the dark.*

JUSTICE. Come forward, Mrs Mary Middleton.

The next matron comes out of the dark, MARY MIDDLETON.

Lay your right hand upon the Book.

MARY *lays her left hand on the bible.* COOMBES *whispers in her ear, and she changes it for her right.*

The same oath / which your fore-matron has taken on her part, you shall well and truly observe and keep on your own respective part. So help you God. Kiss the book.

MARY. Mary Middleton. Wife to Amos Middleton. I do not know what else to tell you except we have five children and there is a tankard in our house that is haunted. It flies across the room sometimes unbidden but I am the only one to have seen it and my husband says he will not throw out a good tankard on my account.

MARY *kisses the book and goes back into the dark.*

JUSTICE. Come forward, Mrs Helen Ludlow.

The next matron comes out of the dark, HELEN LUDLOW.

Lay your right hand upon the Book. The same oath / which your fore-matron has taken on her part, you shall well and truly observe and keep on your own respective part. So help you God. Kiss the book.

HELEN. I am Helen Ludlow, my husband Tom works as a draper. When he proposed he gave me two petticoats and six handkerchiefs. I enjoy the pursuits of rug-work and macramé and have miscarried twelve times in eight years. One child, a boy, born dead. Sometimes Tom makes me laugh so much I think my stays will snap.

HELEN kisses the book and goes back into the dark.

JUSTICE. Come forward, Mrs Emma Jenkins.

The next matron comes out of the dark, EMMA JENKINS.

Lay your right hand upon the Book. The same oath / which your fore-matron has taken on her part, you shall well and truly observe and keep on your own respective part. So help you God. Kiss the book.

EMMA. Mrs Emma Jenkins, wife of Walter, mother to William. We have a shop selling dry goods, a chimney that smokes and a drain at the front of our house that has a foul odour. My son weighed twelve pounds when he was born but we get along very well now.

EMMA wipes the book with her handkerchief, kisses it and goes back into the dark.

JUSTICE. Come forward, Mrs Ann Lavender.

The next matron comes out of the dark, ANN LAVENDER.

Lay your right hand upon the Book. The same oath / which your fore-matron has taken on her part, you shall well and truly observe and keep on your own respective part. So help you God. Kiss the book.

ANN. My name is Ann Lavender, without an E. I was christened with one, but my husband felt me more elegant without it. We moved here recently to raise our four daughters in peasant honesty. William is a poet and had a desire to share the housework equally and take many long solitary walks. He has been very successful at the latter.

ANN *kisses the book and goes back into the dark.*

JUSTICE. Come forward, Mrs Sarah Smith.

The next matron comes out of the dark, SARAH SMITH.

Lay your right hand upon the Book. The same oath / which your fore-matron has taken on her part, you shall well and truly observe and keep on your own respective part. So help you God. Kiss the book.

SARAH SMITH. Sarah Smith. I was born in 1676, I have had twenty-one children and three husbands, all very satisfactory. Until last year I could stand on my hands for a full minute.

SARAH SMITH *kisses the book and goes back into the dark.*

JUSTICE. Come forward, Mrs Margaret Carter.

The next matron comes out of the dark, PEG CARTER.

Lay your right hand upon the Book. The same oath / which your fore-matron has taken on her part, you shall well and truly observe and keep on your own respective part. So help you God. Kiss the book.

PEG. Peg Carter, my husband is David who is gardener to the Wax family, after his father and his grandfather before him. This last year he has planted a Judas tree, lilacs, and dahlias in blue and gold pots. He is a fine man and knows many things such as hanging a hog's hoof to catch earwigs and also there is this thing he is able to do with his tongue which I find very amenable.

PEG *kisses the book and goes back into the dark.*

JUSTICE. Come forward, Mrs Sarah Hollis.

The next matron comes out of the dark, SARAH HOLLIS.

Lay your right hand upon the Book. The same oath / which your fore-matron has taken on her part, you shall well and truly observe and keep on your own respective part. So help you God. Kiss the book.

Pause. SARAH HOLLIS *beams out benignly but says nothing.*

Mrs Hollis, I must hear your oath.

Pause.

Mrs Hollis.

KITTY *comes on, apologetic.*

KITTY. Uh, she doesnae speak your Honour. She's not spoke for – wassit? Twenty years at least, since she had her Lucas. She went into labour quite full of chatter but she's been entirely speechless since.

JUSTICE. How does she get by?

KITTY. Quite well. I'd say, wouldn't you darl?

She looks at SARAH HOLLIS, SARAH HOLLIS *nods in agreement.*

Yes, she says quite well.

JUSTICE. Well. Perhaps if Mrs Hollis might give me a sign she –

SARAH HOLLIS *nods and beams.*

KITTY. Aye, she's nodding.

JUSTICE. Thank you Mrs Hollis. So help you God. Kiss the Book.

SARAH HOLLIS *kisses the book and goes back into the dark.*

Come forward… um… Mrs Katherine Givens.

KITTY. That's me.

JUSTICE. Lay your right hand upon the Book. The same oath / which your fore-matron has taken on her part, you shall well and truly observe and keep on your own respective part. So help you God. Kiss the book.

KITTY. Kitty Givens, come down from Oban. Six children. Four that lived. I do not love the English but the weather is tolerable.

KITTY *kisses the book and goes back into the dark.*

JUSTICE. Come forward, Mrs Judith Brewer.

The next matron comes out of the dark, JUDITH BREWER.

Lay your right hand upon the Book. The same oath / which your fore-matron has taken on her part, you shall well and truly observe and keep on your own respective part. So help you God. Kiss the book.

JUDITH. Judith Brewer. I met my Peter when a boy nailed us together as we admired the Twelfth Night cakes in the window of a pastry-cook in Norwich. I find myself in the midst of the dodging time and though I am wholly fond of my husband I have lately had wild dreams concerning a young ploughman that has lost his shirt. In a rain-storm. Sometimes I am seized by a hot, ungovernable rage, so though it be March I hope the other ladies will consent to having the windows open.

JUDITH *kisses the book and goes back into the dark.*

JUSTICE. Come forward, Mrs Elizabeth Luke.

ELIZABETH LUKE *comes out of the dark.*

Lay your right hand upon the Book. The same oath / which your fore-matron has taken on her part, you shall well and truly observe and keep on your own respective part. So help you God. Kiss the book.

ELIZABETH *hesitates.*

Kiss the Book, Mrs Luke.

Pause.

Mrs / Luke.

ELIZABETH. Forgive me. I am afraid.

JUSTICE. Mr Coombes the bailiff will be present, and the prisoner bound, she cannot hurt you.

ELIZABETH. I am not afraid of the prisoner. I am afraid that if the girl is in the early months, that may be impossible to know for sure, and yet you ask us to make a judgment that may see her hanged. How much time is allowed us?

JUSTICE. As long as is necessary. An hour should suffice.

ELIZABETH. An hour?

JUSTICE. If the child has quickened it will be readily apparent to you.

ELIZABETH. How?

JUSTICE. In… ways.

ELIZABETH. There are no ways.

JUSTICE. I am referring / to –

ELIZABETH. No. There is no clean verdict to be had here, we will be twelve women walking on a carpet of opinion as if that were fact. You give us an hour to make a decision that must be lived with for an eternity.

Pause.

JUSTICE. The matrons are waiting, Mrs Luke.

ELIZABETH *hesitates. Then kisses the book and goes into the dark.*
COOMBES *comes out of the dark and stands before the* JUSTICE.

Mr Coombes. You shall well and truly keep this jury of matrons without meat, drink, fire and candle. You shall not suffer any person but the prisoner to speak unto them, nor you yourself unless it be to ask them if they are agreed of their verdict. So help you God. Kiss the Book.

COOMBES *kisses the book and goes back into the dark. The sound of the butter churn stops.*

5. MEAT, DRINK, FIRE, CANDLE

A cold bare room above the courthouse. It is gloomy. No fire lit although one is laid.

The MATRONS, *except for* ELIZABETH, *are gathered. They chatter, gossiping, laughing, a hum of noise, above which rises the voice of* EMMA JENKINS.

EMMA. Look at that. Dirty skirting. In a court of law, that makes you want to weep, doesn't that? Sarah. Sarah. Sarah. Sarah.

SARAH SMITH looks.

Not you, Sarah Smith, Sarah Hollis.

SARAH HOLLIS looks, she shows her.

Dirty skirting, does that not make you want to weep? Who cleans for them? Who keeps house for the law? That want a good old fye-out, that do, that's dutty as a byre.

SARAH HOLLIS shakes out a handkerchief, spits on it and starts wiping.

And oh my saints, that *floor*! I would not slaughter a pig on that floor, what are you doing Judith Brewer?

JUDITH is opening the window with difficulty, it is stiff. She is sweating.

JUDITH. That's a little close in here, is it not?

A cheer goes up from the crowd outside as they see the window open.

EMMA. It is not! That is freezing, shut that! Shut it!

JUDITH. I do think I would be more comfortable / if

EMMA. Shut. It.

JUDITH shuts the window. Sits down and wipes her neck with a handkerchief.

KITTY. What's the matter?

HELEN. Are you sick?

JUDITH. Only warmer than I want to be.

EMMA. Ice on the rafters this morning, she wants the window open!

CHARLOTTE. She suffers. Let her.

EMMA looks at CHARLOTTE.

EMMA. Beg pardon, we've not met.

CHARLOTTE. Mrs Charlotte Cary. I am visiting from Colchester. My husband was Colonel Samuel Cary, of the 40th Regiment. I believe I am to act as fore-matron.

Pause. EMMA adjusts her deportment, realising she is speaking to a superior.

EMMA. What a cheerful hat. Mrs Emma Jenkins. Very pleased to make your acquaintance.

EMMA curtsies, CHARLOTTE bobs back. KITTY and HANNAH stifle a laugh.

JUDITH. Who?

CHARLOTTE. Excuse me?

JUDITH. Who you visiting?

,

CHARLOTTE. A friend.

ANN. My sister lives at Colchester. St John's Street, do you know it?

CHARLOTTE turns to look at ANN. Pause.

CHARLOTTE. Yes.

EMMA. Don't *crowd* her, Ann! Mrs Cary, won't you take your ease?

EMMA pulls out a chair for CHARLOTTE and sits beside her.

MARY. How long will they keep us, do you think?

EMMA. As long as it takes. I am glad to do my duty to the parish, Mrs Cary.

HELEN. But the office is a painful one, Emma.

EMMA. Painful? Why?

HELEN. To have such power over another life, I find that very discomforting.

EMMA. Do you? I don't, a lot of bodies in this parish would be better off if I had a little power over them. As it is they give their agency to the gin bottle and pass water on my clean step, and the only time anyone consults me on anything is when we are wheeled in for this carnival.

ANN. I have never performed the duty before, have you?

EMMA. Six times. They are invariably lying.

JUDITH. Six times?

EMMA. We lived in London before we came here. There are many more hangings in London. The climate is altogether more criminal.

KITTY. There's more to steal. S'where the money is. They deserve to get robbed.

SARAH SMITH. How do you like our town, Mrs Cary? I ent never left so I am always keen to get an outsider's view on it.

CHARLOTTE. It seems very pleasant.

SARAH SMITH. Oh it is. When nobody's being murdered.

PEG. Hush Mrs Smith! You do know it is usually a wholly civilised place! (*To* CHARLOTTE.) There is a flitch of bacon given as a prize every year to the most happily married couple.

KITTY *and* HANNAH *stifle a groan.*

CHARLOTTE. What a charming tradition.

PEG. Yes, isn't it?

Pause. PEG waits for a question that does not come.

Yes, that is voted on by the whole town. Every household participates.

Pause.

It is a wholly great honour to be the winner.

KITTY. I cannot abide this, just tell her who it was.

PEG. Oh, I'm sure Mrs Cary isn't at all interested / in local

CHARLOTTE. Who was the winner / this year?

PEG. Well actually my husband David and I have won it for two years now.

CHARLOTTE. Oh really?

PEG. Yes.

CHARLOTTE. My congratulations.

PEG. Thank you. It is a lot of bacon.

ELIZABETH *enters*.

ELIZABETH. Ladies.

HANNAH. * Lizzy!

KITTY. * Thank the Lord.

JUDITH. How you going, my little old mawther?

Chatter as the MATRONS, excepting CHARLOTTE and EMMA, flock towards her.

ELIZABETH. I ain't fell apart yet. Peg, how you getting on?

PEG. I am ready to murder someone myself!

ELIZABETH. That won't be long now then.

KITTY. We did not think to see you here today.

ELIZABETH. Mr Coombes came for me. Ann, you look tired.

ANN. Harriet is teething.

ELIZABETH. Have you tried her with laudanum yet?

ANN. I gave her ten drops last night.

ELIZABETH. Try fifteen, see where that gets you. Have you all been here since this morning?

HANNAH. We only come to watch the trial, we did not know we'd be called into service.

PEG. My hands, feel my hands.

ELIZABETH *rubs* PEG*'s hands, warming them for her.*

ELIZABETH. Are you not here of your own free will then?

EMMA. I am.

KITTY. She is.

ANN. The rest of us

SARAH SMITH. They locked the doors.

KITTY. They would not let us out.

HANNAH. The moment the wretch made her plea, Kitty and I saw the way the wind was blowing and tried to run –

ANN. All of us did.

EMMA. I didn't.

PEG. Such a rush of ladies hastening to quit the court.

ELIZABETH. And here you are, them as did not rush fast enough.

MARY *coughs, hawks up some phlegm.*

Mary, it is good to see you mawther, how are you?

MARY. Truth be told Lizzy, I am very vexed.

ELIZABETH. Oh dear, why is that?

MARY. I have a field of leeks must be pulled by night. Will the judgment take very long do you think?

ELIZABETH. The judgment has been passed. We are called only to consult upon the sentence, was that – has no one made that clear to you?

MARY. Oh. Yep. Right you are.

>

Lizzy, I been wanting to ask…

MARY *pulls* ELIZABETH *aside*.

that treatment you give me last year.

ELIZABETH. The plaster of motherwort?

MARY. No. No. No, the other. In the. On the bed. When you. You know. With your hand and the. Ointment and the. (*Sotto*.) Rubbing.

ELIZABETH. Culpeper's remedy, yes, very reliable, did you feel a benefit?

MARY. Yes, I did, I did, I did feel, that was, that was a very helpful evacuation, that was.

ELIZABETH. Very refreshing.

MARY. That's it. That's exactly it. Got all them, evil humours out that did.

ELIZABETH. I'm glad you saw an effect.

MARY. Oh yes I did, yes.

>

Yes, howsomever, I do feel lately there is quite a, quite an accumulation of Evil in me again. I dunno where that's come from but. Best to uh. Best to get that out, don't you think?

ELIZABETH. I do. You come and see me next Tuesday.

MARY. I will very much look forward to that, Lizzy.

JUDITH. Is today not your Great Wash, mawther?

ELIZABETH *turns to* JUDITH, *peers at her, feels her cheek*.

ELIZABETH. That is. Judith you's warm, shall we have this window open?

ELIZABETH *strides across the room, throws open the window. The sound of an angry, baying crowd outside. They are all arrested by it.*

CHARLOTTE. Have none of them employment to go to?

ANN. They are wild, are they not?

JUDITH. They had thought to see her swinging by now.

ELIZABETH. They are ahead of themselves.

EMMA. Oh no. She'll piss when she can't whistle. Sooner or later.

CHARLOTTE. She must look to the Welkin. There is no earthly help for her now.

ELIZABETH *studies* CHARLOTTE.

ELIZABETH. Beg pardon, I never caught your name.

EMMA *rushes forward, with a great show of manners.*

EMMA. Allow me to, Mrs Charlotte Cary, Mrs Elizabeth Luke, Mrs Cary is fore-matron of our jury, visiting our province from Colchester / and

ELIZABETH. Our what?

EMMA. Our province.

ELIZABETH. Our what?

EMMA. Our province.

ELIZABETH. Ohhh.

EMMA. And Mrs Luke is the local midwife.

ELIZABETH. I also keep the town whites bag so if you dirty your linens while you're here, or you've bloodstains you can't shift, knock me up.

CHARLOTTE. I certainly shall.

ELIZABETH. Soak it in salt and cold water.

CHARLOTTE. Beg pardon?

ELIZABETH. That's how you shift a bloodstain. Salt and cold water. And there is our help.

CHARLOTTE *looks at the others and laughs, baffled and unnerved.*

JUDITH (*quiet*). Pack it in, mawther.

ELIZABETH *looks at* JUDITH. *A tiny nod.*

ELIZABETH. No, I was only saying, we might help the prisoner.

CHARLOTTE. Help her how? She cannot be helped. She is an animal.

ELIZABETH. Her claim may be true.

The MATRONS, *apart from* ELIZABETH *and* HELEN, *laugh.*

HANNAH. You have not seen her Lizzy, she is thin as reeds.

KITTY. Very plain.

ANN. Bovine.

KITTY. She stood in the dock, completely silent

JUDITH. did not say a thing

CHARLOTTE. but made impertinent expressions at the comments of the magistrate

PEG. and when Lord Wax took the stand she, well she was

KITTY. flirting. With a father in grief. Completely unbidden.

ELIZABETH. Perhaps not completely. She worked in the household, did she not?

KITTY. So?

ELIZABETH. So John Wax takes it as his personal duty to fuck all the servant girls, does he not?

The MATRONS *smother gasps.*

HELEN. Lizzy, are you, are you quite well?

ELIZABETH. Even if we support her claim, that will not mean a pardon. She will still be transported.

EMMA. Lizzy she is lying! And she will hang, and when that rabble are let loose there'll be little left for the surgeons.

ELIZABETH. Surgeons? What surgeons?

ANN. The Justice was not content to merely hang her, he sentenced she should be anatomised afterwards.

The MATRONS *shudder, and stand in silence, listening to the crowd.*

JUDITH *suddenly starts forward.*

JUDITH. Enough.

She shuts the window. Fans herself.

ELIZABETH. Have they fed you?

KITTY. Did they not tell you? No food, no water, no fire, no candle.

ELIZABETH *produces the bread.*

ELIZABETH. Here. Eat that quickly, before Mr Coombes comes in.

The MATRONS *fall upon the bread, eating hungrily.*

HELEN. Elizabeth, may I speak, uh, privately, / you know

ELIZABETH. Of course Helen.

They separate themselves from the group.

HELEN. I think there has been some confusion.

ELIZABETH. Yes.

HELEN. I should not be here.

ELIZABETH. No.

HELEN. I am not qualified. I tried to explain to Mr Coombes only he was in such a rush.

ELIZABETH. You did not tell the magistrate when you swore your oath?

HELEN. I intended to, only... I wanted someone here to speak for the girl. We lived next to her parents' house for some time. That was an unquiet home. They kept a great number of ferrets and the children were always dirty. The stepfather, Francis Cobb was, I do not like to speak ill but, well –

ELIZABETH. He was a queer bitch.

HELEN. Yes.

,

I – yes and the brother, Silas, too but Sally doted on him and would take the blame for all his misdeeds. The breaking of a window. The theft of a ham. Small things, but I wonder if that is what happened here with Thomas McKay. If you had seen her during the trial... the way she looked at him... it was... a stupid look. But full of love.

We none of us know what happened that night except Sally herself and she will say nothing. There was not a single person to speak for her in that courtroom and now she thinks to save herself with a lie that no one will believe. But I do not think she did it, Lizzy. I am sure of it.

HANNAH *and* KITTY *come over.*

KITTY. Are we putting theories? Cos we've one –

HANNAH. Justice says there is no possibility it was an accident, right? Cos of the amount of force, you see / but

KITTY. but what if, cos you've heard about this comet that Mr Halley has predicted?

ELIZABETH. I have.

KITTY. Right so you know that's just a fucken big lump of rock, right?

HANNAH. Flying through the sky

KITTY. Flying through the sky, exactly and all of us waiting to see it go over but / what if

HANNAH. *but what if that already went, the night Alice Wax died, and we missed it.*

They both beam at her, triumphant. Pause.

ELIZABETH. So what if it did?

KITTY. So, d'you not? Very well, so she's going quite a speed is she not? And say she flies over Alice Wax, taking a midnight stroll / and

HANNAH. and a lump falls off her

KITTY. and a lump falls off her. Huge lump.

HANNAH. and now that's falling

KITTY. hundreds of miles that's hurtling to earth, gathering speed

HANNAH. and force

KITTY. gathering speed and force, faster and faster and when it finally falls, what's between her and the ground?

HANNAH. little Alice Wax

KITTY. little Alice Wax's poor wee head.

Pause.

ELIZABETH. It is a very vivid proposal.

KITTY. Thank you.

ELIZABETH. But not a little unlikely, do you not think?

HANNAH. To say a thing is unlikely does not make it impossible.

KITTY. True, Mary Middleton's husband's prick is shaped like a question mark and yet they have five children.

MARY *hears her name and looks up.*

MARY. What's that?

KITTY. Nothing pet, eat your bread.

HELEN. Could I ask a question?

KITTY. Yes darlin'.

HELEN. I think that's a very interesting proposal, but how d'you explain Sally being found with a hammer in the middle of the night?

HANNAH *and* KITTY *look at one another.*

HANNAH. Hanging a…

KITTY. Hanging a picture mebbe.

ELIZABETH. And how did Alice end up in two sacks?

Pause.

KITTY. S'very easy to pick an idea to pieces.

HANNAH. We was only trying to think charitably of the wretch.

ELIZABETH. You are good gals, and that's a wholly well-thought scheme, thank you.

HANNAH *and* KITTY *move away, mollified.* ELIZABETH *kisses* HELEN.

I am grateful to see you here Helen. And you have laboured longer than any of us. I am sure the other ladies would not see you turned out, now come and eat.

ELIZABETH *and* HELEN *rejoin the group, now seated.*

MARY. Where is she then? That's wrong, that is, keeping us waiting when we've work to do.

KITTY. Did you not mention your leeks to the Justice then, Mary?

MARY. No. Why, you think I should?

CHARLOTTE. I expect they must ensure the prisoner is properly bound before they allow her into the company of respectable women like ourselves.

EMMA. I heard that last year Sally sold some of her teeth to Mrs Evesham, and shortly after Mrs Evesham had them struck out again, complaining that they made all food taste bitter. She has had replacements made instead in porcelain. What do you think to that?

JUDITH. I think Mrs Evesham should not take so much sugar, the puff-guts, she might still have her old teeth and not need to buy new ones.

ANN. Mrs Brewer, that isn't kind. Mrs Evesham gives great charity to the poor of the parish.

PEG. So? I hate the poor. They sell their teeth and ask for pity.

ANN. But there is no work for them. Their lives are very desolate.

PEG. Work, there is work, they can sweep crossings and black shoes, can they not? That is work.

A loud bang on the door.

JUDITH. Come in if you're good looking.

The MATRONS *laugh. The door opens.* COOMBES *enters.*

That'll do. Hello bor, how you getting on?

COOMBES *counts the* MATRONS.

SARAH SMITH. What you gone and done to your wing, there?

MARY. Fell off Miss Gooch's roof, he did, I saw it.

JUDITH. What'd he do that for? What d'you do that for?

COOMBES *goes out again.* SALLY *is pushed into the room. A pillowcase over her head. The* MATRONS *stand.* COOMBES *returns, removes the pillowcase and locks the door behind her.*

SALLY. Ladies.

She curtsies. The MATRONS *murmur a greeting back. Pause.*

ANN. Are we allowed to touch the, her?

Pause.

Mr Coombes?

CHARLOTTE. Mr Coombes is not allowed to speak to us except to ask our verdict.

EMMA. He cannot stay silent the whole time?

HANNAH. He will if he knows what's good for him.

ANN. But he listens.

KITTY. Oh aye, Mr Coombes is always listening. He's all ears, is Mr Coombes.

KITTY, HANNAH *and* PEG *giggle at some private joke.*

ANN. But what if we've a question to put to him?

SARAH SMITH. For example, are we allowed to touch the prisoner?

CHARLOTTE. Mrs Jenkins, you have done this before, what is your opinion?

EMMA. I think, if it is in aid of discerning if she is with child.

HELEN. And we do not harm her.

PEG. I'm not touching her. She's a pollution.

KITTY. Aye I can smell her from here.

JUDITH. She just wants washing.

ELIZABETH. Hello Sally.

Pause.

SALLY. Hello.

ELIZABETH. You don't remember me do you? When did we last meet? Five years ago at least, was that not? You were courting with one of the Akas boys, what was his name?

'

SALLY. Oliver.

ELIZABETH. Oliver, that's it, you were besotted. What happened to him?

SALLY. Married one of the Ling girls. Bungay way.

ELIZABETH. I am sorry to hear that.

CHARLOTTE. Is this a tea party? Shall I ring for hot water?

ELIZABETH. I was only putting the girl at her ease.

ANN. I don't think we should talk to her any more than necessary.

ELIZABETH. Very well. Shall we begin?

CHARLOTTE. Let us have the older ladies first.

JUDITH. Cats before kittens.

MARY. I am twenty-five, is that old or young?

KITTY. You wait your turn with us, love.

The older MATRONS (SARAH SMITH, SARAH HOLLIS, CHARLOTTE, ELIZABETH, EMMA, HELEN *and* JUDITH) *stand around* SALLY *and examine her belly.*

ELIZABETH. There is a swelling, to my eye.

EMMA. Not to mine.

CHARLOTTE. Nor to mine. Mrs Brewer?

JUDITH. Yeah, I'd say there's a pod on her, what d'you reckon Sarah?

SARAH SMITH. There's a pod, don't mean she's quickened. Someone have to feel it.

She looks around. No one comes forward. SARAH HOLLIS *sighs. Puts her hand on* SALLY'*s belly. Waits. Shakes her head.*

Nuffen. Mrs Hollis?

She looks at SARAH HOLLIS, *who shrugs.*

You girls, come and see.

The younger matrons come over, HANNAH, PEG, KITTY, MARY *and* ANN.

HANNAH. I ent wholly sure.

ANN. I think I see something. She is a little round here.

PEG. No, that is only how she carries her fat, she is gotch-gutted, my sister is the same.

KITTY. I dunno.

MARY. Me neither.

ANN. Tell us your symptoms.

HANNAH. Are you dizzy?

SARAH SMITH. Do you have a misery in your stomach? Does it cast off what you put in it?

EMMA. Do you feel too tired to blink?

KITTY. Does everything taste of onions?

CHARLOTTE. Are you troubled by sour belchings?

PEG. Are you thirsty? Sweating?

MARY. Do you piss more than you drink?

JUDITH. What about your dairy, is it tender?

ANN. Have you lost all desire to eat meat?

HELEN. Are you very warm?

PEG. Or cold, I am ever so cold.

ANN. Do you feel sometimes merry and sometimes sad with no cause?

SARAH SMITH. Do you have a sore throat?

KITTY. It's March and it's rafty,[1] we've all sore throats.

SARAH SMITH. Twenty-one children I've had, all of them started with a sore throat. One time that turned out I had smallpox instead, I nearly died but I was so relieved.

MARY. Do you have a great desire to eat strange things, such as, for example, a piece of your husband's buttocks?

SALLY. I've got the shits. And when I lay down to sleep at night a great crack rents the sky and angels come flooding out of it.

,

---

1. Raw, damp weather.

SARAH SMITH. I never heard that one.

MARY. My granny saw an angel.

HANNAH. She never.

MARY. She did. Last time the comet came. It flapped its wings so hard the thatch come off the roof and that night, she gave birth to a very hairy boy with two thumbs on one hand.

,

HELEN. So what now?

JUDITH. When I was a girl, you wanted to know if you were poisoned before you saw the swelling, you went to Lally Fletcher.

SARAH SMITH. Ah.

JUDITH. You remember Lally?

SARAH SMITH. I do. Her husband used to come to our house to play cards.

JUDITH. Right well you know then, Lally was the one to go to. She'd tell you if you was or you wasn't, boy or girl, and whether it would come quick or slow.

ANN. And was she often right?

JUDITH. She was never wrong. She was the one for getting rid of warts too. She'd say, 'Let me look at your wart', and you'd show it to her, and then she'd say, 'how many have you got?'

Pause. The MATRONS *wait. Eventually:*

KITTY. And?

JUDITH. What?

KITTY. What she do then?

JUDITH. Nothing. Week or so later, that wart'd be gone.

MARY. No.

JUDITH *nods*.

JUDITH. Lally was the one for warts.

KITTY. What, so she *enquired* it away?

JUDITH. I don't know what she did, that's her business, my business is, did three warts on the back of my hand disappear six days after Lally looked at them, yes they did, and did she not tell me before I knew myself that I was quick with my Catherine, yes she did, and did she not tell me she was to be a girl, yes she did, and did she not tell me she would come out like a greased weasel in under three hours, yes she did. However, Lally is now dead from a cartwheel to the head she did not see coming so what are we gonna do about this one?

CHARLOTTE. We might see if she has milk?

ELIZABETH. She is still in the early months, a lack of milk would not be proof she is lying.

CHARLOTTE. But you accept that the presence of it would settle the claim?

ELIZABETH. Certainly.

HANNAH. My last, the milk never come in until two weeks after the birth. I was reliant on Kitty to nurse him.

KITTY. I had more than enough, I was pleased to do it.

SARAH SMITH. Sometimes mine came in at six months, sometimes not till much later, you couldn't call it dependable.

MARY. Oh, since my second, mine has always come with the quickening and is very yellow. Some years ago our cat licked up some drops of it from the floor and three hours later it *died* but Amos thought the events to be unrelated.

ELIZABETH. Mr Coombes, will you step outside please?

COOMBES *shakes his head*.

Very well then turn your back please, and face the door.

Pause.

Mr Coombes we must undress the prisoner, I believe Mrs Coombes, though she be in Lowestoft, would prefer you face the door.

The MATRONS *laugh.* COOMBES *faces the door.*

Thank you.

ANN. Who will perform the examination?

HELEN. Elizabeth should do it.

CHARLOTTE. No. Mrs Luke is too disposed towards the girl, she may have some trick for conjuring the milk.

ELIZABETH *looks at* CHARLOTTE.

Do not be insulted Mrs Luke, I have observed your heart is tender, that is a compliment to you.

ELIZABETH. Yes but I am a midwife not a magician, Mrs Cary.

CHARLOTTE. Nonetheless.

ELIZABETH. Kitty, perhaps you would / like to

MARY. I do think we could hurry this along a mite, I do.

EMMA. Oh, do we bore you?

KITTY. She's on about her leeks again. Come on, / let's

KITTY *reaches out to open* SALLY*'s clothes.* SALLY *smacks her hands away.*

SALLY. Fuck / off!

KITTY. Oi!

COOMBES *starts towards* SALLY *but* ELIZABETH *holds him off.*

ELIZABETH. * It is alright Mr Coombes!

SALLY. * Turn around! Turn around!

ELIZABETH *holds them apart.*

ELIZABETH. Sally, please – Mr Coombes / if you'd just

SALLY. I want him turned around!

ELIZABETH. TURN AROUND MR COOMBES.

CHARLOTTE. For God's sakes man, do as you're told!

Reluctantly, COOMBES *turns around again.*

ELIZABETH. Sally. Kitty was only / trying to

SALLY. She tried to touch my tit!

KITTY. Oh for / Christ's sakes.

HELEN. It's only ladies here, dear.

SARAH SMITH. Kitty will not hurt you.

EMMA. Not like a rope round your neck will.

EMMA laughs.

SALLY. There is milk, I have seen it, let me out of these bonds, I will show you myself.

CHARLOTTE. You are a criminal. Don't think as how you shall domineer here.

SALLY. Let me out!

ELIZABETH. Sally, we cannot do that.

SALLY. 'Sally, we cannot do that', why fucking not?

CHARLOTTE. We do not have the authority.

HANNAH. Or the key.

CHARLOTTE. Or the key.

Pause. SALLY *sighs.*

SALLY. Warm your hands then.

,

WARM YOUR HANDS I WILL NOT HAVE FRIGID PAWS ON ME

The MATRONS *rub their hands together to warm them up.* SALLY *glances at* COOMBES *to make sure his back is still turned.*

Mr Coombes, I am about to give my privities an airing, but I have my eye on you, and if you make even a quarter-turn towards me I will kick your cock into your kidneys, that's if I can find him.

KITTY *comes forward.*

Not you.

KITTY *makes a sound of exasperation.*

PEG. Quickest if Lizzy does it.

SALLY. Not her neither.

ANN. Mrs Luke is a midwife of many years, Sally.

SALLY. I know that. I know all about Mrs Luke, I smelt her before I come in the room. She is ignorant and her nails are never clean. She does not wash her hands and last year she had Mrs Fry in labour for five days and only a tar-faced little dead thing to show for it at the end.

HELEN. Sally, Mrs Luke has been / kind to you

SALLY. AND she had loose bowels for many days after, from all / the caudle she had her drink

HELEN. there is no reason to speak to her so harshly!

SALLY. and her cunt was ruined shut up Helen what are you even doing here everyone knows you're barren.

HELEN *sits down.*

If I had wealth, I'd follow fashion and have a doctor attend me, a MAN who knows what he's doing, not some village woman, some rabbit-catcher by candlelight, grubby-aproned big-hipped blood-letter going from laying out corpses to lying-in chambers, death still under her fingernails, multiplying, I DON'T KNOW WHY YOU ARE ALL LOOKING AT ME LIKE THAT, I have heard half of you say as much behind her back.

ELIZABETH. Sally, I know you are frightened and you are upset / but

SALLY. AND MRS FRY CANNOT LAUGH BUT SHE PISSES HERSELF.

ELIZABETH. I am trying to save your life.

SALLY. Ahhh. That's nice.

ELIZABETH. You do not want my help?

SALLY. I do not need anything from you. I want one of you nice old cats should do it. You, chatterbox.

She gestures to SARAH HOLLIS. SARAH HOLLIS *looks at* ELIZABETH.

ELIZABETH. Go on Sarah Hollis.

SARAH HOLLIS *approaches* SALLY *tentatively.*

SALLY. Wait, put your hand on my cheek, let me feel if your blood is warm.

SARAH HOLLIS *puts her hand gently on* SALLY'*s cheek. Pause. Her hand remains.*
SALLY *breathes. Closes her eyes.*

Some time.

SALLY *opens her eyes. Nods.*
SARAH HOLLIS *loosens* SALLY'*s stays, puts a handkerchief inside* SALLY'*s shift, reaches in and begins to try to squeeze milk from her breasts. The* MATRONS *watch.*

I have had milk come, but not regular you know. And not in great quantities so. I mean to say I have seen it but... not every day.

,

All I am saying is, is if that didn't come directly that is no cause to... I mean you could not call that proof... I am an irregular woman. And a body is not a machine, is it? Milk is... it don't do as it is told, it comes and it goes. It ent governable. Sometimes that just takes a minute to... to... to... to

SALLY *smothers a sound of discomfort.*

ELIZABETH. Does she hurt you?

SALLY. No, do it harder.

> SARAH HOLLIS *obeys*. SALLY *tolerates the pain*.

> *The other* MATRONS *take a seat as they wait*. JUDITH *fans herself, she is warm, but the room is cold and the others shiver and pull their shawls around them*.

ANN. You know, I do not believe she even did it.

HELEN. Nor I. Lizzy, wasn't I just / saying

EMMA. Fred Poppy saw her set fire to the girl's hair!

ANN. He saw something burn by candlelight, when we know his eyesight to be poor.

EMMA. I don't know that.

KITTY. Well I watched him raise his cap to a grandfather clock on the way out, / so

CHARLOTTE. And the dress, what about the dress?

EMMA. Exactly Mrs Cary, an excellent question, what of the dress? Covered in blood that was, you saw it.

SARAH SMITH. All of us saw it.

ANN. Yes but if you look at the facts, this Mr McKay was guilty of a number of quite hideous crimes up and down the country long before he met Sally. And she strikes me as the sort of girl who does not know to run away during knock down ginger and is left alone on the doorstep though she never banged on the door. If I had been permitted to join the jury proper, I would have had a great many questions / to put to

CHARLOTTE. This is not what is asked of us, Mrs Lavender.

ANN. No, we are not asked anything except to give confected opinions upon a science in which we are none of us scholars.

EMMA. We have suffered to bear children.

PEG. Most of us.

JUDITH. Yes, and I was six months with my Edward before I knew of it.

KITTY. Get away!

JUDITH. Excuse me, I was. I did not show much even at the end, and my curse was never regular.

MARY. Last year I bled every day from Christmas till Shrove Tuesday.

ANN. At least you did not have to worry about getting in pod.

MARY. Yes but Amos would not be a husband to me at all during that time.

EMMA. 'One of the properties of a good man is not to lie with a menstruous woman'. Ezekiel 18:18.

CHARLOTTE. Mrs Jenkins is right, you are lucky to have a husband who gives such regard to cleanliness.

MARY. Well he were happy to be husband to a region I think considerably less clean, but if you say so. Anyway after that I did not have my flowers at all till June and the blood was not red or brown but a sort of purple colour and clotted. Smelt, too. Not bad. Like metal.

PEG (*reproving*). Mary.

She throws her eyes to COOMBES. MARY *sees him, laughs.*

MARY. Oh, I am sorry Mr Coombes, I quite forgot you was there.

KITTY. Is that not what Mrs Coombes said on her wedding night?

KITTY, PEG, MARY *and* HANNAH *laugh.*

ELIZABETH. Are your flowers regular, Sally?

SALLY. Not since the first child I lost, no.

HELEN. How many have / you

SALLY. With this present child, it will be three.

SARAH SMITH. Don't talk like that. If that's true then both of you will live.

SALLY. Well I never could keep hold of one before so.

EMMA. Some women can't, their insides are buttered.

JUDITH. Emma.

JUDITH *throws her eyes to* HELEN.

EMMA. I didn't mean anything by it.

ANN. Was the child wanted?

SALLY. It was wanted but not intended. I can't pretend we didn't act to avoid it, only the gentleman did not withdraw when I told him to.

JUDITH. That's not a method you can rely on, they're senseless at the last post. With Mr Brewer I always kept a piece of brick in a handkerchief under the bed, if you time your strike right you can save yourself a lot of trouble in the long run.

Pause. SARAH HOLLIS *continues her attempts.*

KITTY. Lizzy, is it not true that if we kept her water three days, then strained it through a linen, if she's expecting you'd find live worms?

ELIZABETH. It is not. And we do not have three days.

ANN. In Ancient Greece you could pass water onto a bag of barley and if it sprouted then you knew.

HANNAH. But you couldn't eat the barley after.

ANN. No, it was a waste of grain, that's true.

The MATRONS *laugh. Pause.*

HELEN. Peg, I've been thinking all morning, that shawl is just lovely.

PEG. Do you know, I receive so many compliments on this and that's quite the oldest thing I own.

HELEN. What is it, muslin?

PEG. No, it's lawn.

SARAH HOLLIS *takes the handkerchief from inside* SALLY's *shift and examines it.*

CHARLOTTE. Well?

SARAH HOLLIS *shows them that the handkerchief is dry, shakes her head.*

You may turn around Mr Coombes.

COOMBES *turns back to the room.*

SALLY. She was only trying a minute! And her efforts were pale, I shouldn't have chose someone so chicken-breasted, I do not think she knew what to do with a proper pair of churks.

ELIZABETH. Perhaps we could wait a while and try again.

MARY *groans.*

EMMA. She is lying! There is no belly and no milk!

SALLY. Let me have someone not so cow-handed and I will show you!

EMMA. She is a demy-rep!

SALLY. I HAVE NOT BLED IN FOUR MONTHS AND MY TITS HURT.

EMMA. And a thief, she has always been a thief. I myself have been victim to it, nobody cared then only now it is a girl's life has been stolen.

ANN. You claim she has stolen from you in the past?

EMMA. Claim it, I don't claim it, I state it. / It is fact.

SALLY. Oh FUCK ME here we go.

ANN. What did she steal?

EMMA. She had off us six nutmegs.

SALLY. My God, the nutmegs, I knew we would hear about the nutmegs / sooner or later.

SARAH SMITH. I wasn't aware there was a criminal history.

CHARLOTTE. Yes, I do think we should have been apprised of the history.

EMMA. SHE'S A DIRTY PUZZLE.

SALLY. LIAR YOU ARE A LIAR EMMA JENKINS,
I NEVER TOOK YOUR BLOODY NUTMEGS!

ELIZABETH. Is this not immaterial?

CHARLOTTE. It is her moral character.

ELIZABETH. It is a nutmeg!

EMMA. SIX NUTMEGS.

ELIZABETH. BEG PARDON ARE WE DISCUSSING
NUTMEGS OR THE LIFE OF A WOMAN?

Pause. HANNAH *starts to giggle.*

HANNAH. Do anyone

Her giggles keep overtaking her.

Do anyone else hear that

Now she's convulsed with laughter.

JUDITH. She's gone, she has.

SALLY. What's the matter with her?

SARAH SMITH. Dicked in the nob, she is.

HANNAH *gathers herself.*

HANNAH. No, I'm alright, I'm alright. I was only asking if

No, she's gone again.

JUDITH. Steady breaths. Think of suffen sad.

HANNAH. Do anyone else hear... that someone else in this
room... is also one nutmeg short?

A beat. Then in unison the MATRONS *and* SALLY *all look
at* COOMBES.

EMMA. Hannah Rusted you wicked article!

SALLY, PEG, KITTY, MARY, JUDITH, SARAH SMITH,
SARAH HOLLIS *and* ANN *burst out laughing. The rest of
the* MATRONS *are appalled or pretend to be.*

ELIZABETH. That's a load of old squit!

HANNAH. Oh? Then why's his wife run off?

EMMA. That is his *private* affair Hannah! I am horrified –
horrified!

HELEN. Oh leave off Emma. He never even tried to get her
back.

SARAH SMITH. He did.

HELEN. How?

SARAH SMITH. Ask Judith.

They all look at JUDITH, *who becomes very interested in
her lap.*

KITTY. Come, come Mrs Brewer. Look up and speak. Your
muff cannot be that interesting even to Mr Brewer.

JUDITH. No, I don't like to mardle.

HANNAH. Go on!

EMMA. I will not have any part of this.

JUDITH. Emma's right, this ent what we're here to discuss.

PEG/HANNAH/MARY/KITTY. Go on / Tell us / Please Judith.

JUDITH. No, that's no good you putting on parts, I ent saying
nothing.

SALLY. Please.

JUDITH *looks at her for a beat.*

JUDITH. He put an advertisement in the *Norwich Mercury*. My
sister who lives in Tacolneston[2] sent me the clipping.

HELEN. But what did it say?

JUDITH. As I say, I don't like to mardle.

Pause.

SARAH SMITH. Howsomever.

---

2. Pronounced 'Tackleston'.

JUDITH. Howsomever I have it here as it happens.

She takes a letter from the pocket tied to her waist, takes a clipping from the envelope.

EMMA. I am ashamed! Quite ashamed. Mrs Cary, I intend to stop up my ears and eyes until this disgusting show is over, will you join me?

CHARLOTTE. Certainly Mrs Jenkins.

EMMA puts her hands over her ears, closes her eyes, hums. CHARLOTE does not.

CHARLOTTE. Mrs Brewer?

JUDITH (*reading*). 'Whereas Matilda, the wife of me, William Coombes, has absconded to Lowestoft without any cause, notice is hereby given that whoever harbours her will be prosecuted. She is twenty-six years of age, has a round face and dun-coloured hair. Her husband will not be answerable for any debts she may hereafter contract.'

Hard to imagine a heart not melting upon reading that, ent it?

SARAH SMITH. I shouldn't like to live on the coast, I shouldn't. Could be an invasion any minute. Could be ten thousand French soldiers swarmin' into Yarmouth, ready to rape us in our beds.

JUDITH. True, though I do feel that's suffen the editor of the *Norwich Mercury* might give precedence to over Mr Coombes's round-faced wife.

ANN. Besides, I think Mr Pitt has the war in hand.

MARY. Pitt?

ANN. William Pitt.

MARY stares at her.

MARY. Not Willy Pitt with the one big eye who comes round selling fripperies?

KITTY. Yes, that's right Mary, they put him charge of the army.

PEG. Mr Pitt went to Eton College with Lord Wax. They are
dear friends. Mr Pitt came to dine last summer and sent
special compliments to David on the very high quality of his
cucumbers.

HELEN. I do not understand why there must be a war at all.

ANN. To seize power. To take the American territories. To avail
ourselves of the fruits of West Africa and the Caribbean.
To gain an Empire.

MARY. Why d'we want to do that then?

ANN. So that by the end of this century we might be masters of
the world.

CHARLOTTE. Rather than the French.

ANN. Rather than the French, exactly.

PEG. I am not afraid to say it, I hate the French.

JUDITH. I wouldn't say I hate them, but I shouldn't like to be
under them.

MARY. Thing is though, you take all that off someone else,
you're liable for someone to come along and take that back
off you and then where are you? Example, two years in a
row Peg and David won that flitch of bacon. Now let's
suppose next year, they don't win.

PEG *laughs*.

PEG. No, I, I think we will.

MARY. Let's say Helen and Tom win that instead.

PEG *laughs again*.

Then that's a whole year you and David got to live knowing
one time you was the happiest pair in town with so much
bacon you didn't know what to do with it, and now you's
only a gardener's wife eating porridge for supper again with
a baby what won't sleep the night and a smoky chimbley.

PEG. The bacon is really only a symbol, so.

MARY. Now Amos and me, we ent never been the most happily married couple. But we ent killed each other yet. And if we can go on not killing each other for another thirty years, well. Reckon that's good enough for me, and there ent none of that anyone else can rob off us.

SALLY. Thomas said, if someone robs off you, you can rob off them, and if anyone has more than you, that's only cos they've robbed you a long time ago, so you can rob them too. There was a ruby on her finger, with seed pearls all around it.

ELIZABETH. Sally, stop it.

SALLY. Eleven years old and a ruby. What?

Pause. EMMA is still humming with her eyes shut.
CHARLOTTE shakes her gently.

CHARLOTTE. Mrs Jenkins. You may return to us.

EMMA opens her eyes. Surveys the MATRONS.

EMMA. Are we women once again and not pigs?

CHARLOTTE. It is time we took a vote. Those who believe the prisoner to be lying, and not with child, raise your hand.

CHARLOTTE, EMMA, SARAH HOLLIS, HANNAH, KITTY, SARAH SMITH and PEG raise their hands.
CHARLOTTE counts the vote.

And those who believe her to be telling the truth, and with quick child, raise your hand now.

ELIZABETH, ANN, HELEN, MARY and JUDITH raise their hands.

We are split. Seven votes to five.

PEG. But we have the majority.

EMMA. That settles it, to my mind.

ELIZABETH. Surely we must all be in agreement?

MARY. Was that the final count?

EMMA. * Yes.

ELIZABETH. * No.

HELEN. Does no one know if the opinion must be unanimous, or if the Justice demands only a majority?

COOMBES. If I could / just

KITTY. No! You do not speak! It is not your turn to speak!

COOMBES. But

KITTY. Lizzy, tell him!

ELIZABETH. It is the law.

COOMBES. Mrs Luke I

ELIZABETH. It is the law Mr Coombes.

ANN. But surely in the case of such a confusion?

COOMBES. I do think / this is a very particular

KITTY. LIZZY TELL HIM!

CHARLOTTE. What is the confusion? Are these things not set down?

ANN. Mrs Jenkins what is the practice in London?

EMMA. I'm sure seven votes would be quite sufficient there.

ELIZABETH. This is not London.

EMMA. Lizzy, do not take the owl with me, Mrs Lavender / asked my opinion.

MARY. I think I have changed my mind.

CHARLOTTE. It is baffling to me no one has thought to define the terms. Mr Coombes, we have taken a vote. Will you please tell us what it means?

COOMBES. Certainly

ELIZABETH/KITTY/HANNAH/PEG/HELEN/JUDITH. NO.

EMMA. Let the man speak!

KITTY. Mr Coombes is not here to speak!

HANNAH. Mr Coombes is only to see to it we have no food, drink, fire or light, that is all / Mr Coombes is fit for.

MARY. Lizzy, I have changed / my

ELIZABETH. One moment, Mary.

CHARLOTTE. We must have some authority. Speak man!

ELIZABETH. Mr Coombes, if you speak one word I will tell the Justice you have violated the most basic requirements of your position. It is time for you to listen and not to talk, do you understand me?

Pause. COOMBES *opens his mouth. Closes it again.*

MARY *sighs and looks at the darkening sky outside.*

MARY. Getting dark now.

KITTY. MARY DARLING NO ONE CARES A HALF-FARTHING FOR YOUR FUCKING LEEKS.

CHARLOTTE. This is ridiculous. Mr Coombes, if we must be united in our direction to the Justice then... then blink twice.

COOMBES *blinks twice. The* MATRONS, *but for* ELIZABETH, *groan.*

Then either you must persuade us she is telling the truth, or we must convince you she is lying.

MARY. 'Scuse me.

EMMA. I will not be persuaded.

PEG. Nor I.

MARY. 'Scuse me, I did not understand.

CHARLOTTE. You wish to change your vote?

MARY. Yes.

ELIZABETH. Mary, no. Please.

MARY. I had thought that would go the other way. That seemed as though more would be merciful than not, but if that is not the case, that makes no odds to me, if that would help to, to, to, you know

ELIZABETH. what?

MARY. hasten the thing.

ELIZABETH. That will take as much time as that takes Mary.
We are deciding whether to put a woman to death.

,

MARY. Please. That's a very big field, that is. If I ent out there
by three there'll not be enough daylight.

Some of the MATRONS *express exasperation.* ELIZABETH
fights not to hit her.

Anyway, you can tell just looking at her can't you?

ANN. That she isn't with child?

MARY. That she's a liar.

Pause.

CHARLOTTE. So we are now eight to four.

JUDITH. But we must be twelve all-in.

ANN. How do we proceed?

ELIZABETH. Does no one else wish to change their opinion to
give the girl the benefit of the doubt?

EMMA. Why?

ELIZABETH. Why? In truth?

Because she has been sentenced to hang on the word of
a cuckolded husband. Because her mother Janet says she was
not unaccounted for on the night in question but at Janet's
house, weeping and frightened with a bloody nose, a fact
I learnt from the prison laundry maid, cos it was not admitted
to the court. Because every card dealt to her today and for
many years before has been an unkind one, because she has
been sentenced by men pretending to be certain of things of
which they are entirely ignorant, and now we sit here
imitating them, trying to make an ungovernable thing
governable, I do not ask you to like her. I ask you to hope for

her, so that she might know she is worth hoping for. And if you cannot do that for her sake, think instead of the women who will be in this room when that comet comes round again, and how brittle they will think our spirits, how ashamed they will be, that we were given our own dominion and we made it look exactly like the one down there.

She points, meaning the courtroom below.
Pause. Then SALLY blows a raspberry at ELIZABETH's words.
ELIZABETH sits, exhausted.

CHARLOTTE. There is a chill on the air in here. Let us light the fire.

COOMBES *coughs extravagantly to demonstrate this is not permitted.*

HELEN. I don't believe we are allowed to light it. No fire was one / of the

KITTY. Laid isn't it?

JUDITH. I do think we should respect the conventions of the court.

CHARLOTTE. When was the chimney last swept?

EMMA. Some time in the last century, I expect.

JUDITH. Anyway, we have no tinderbox, so

ELIZABETH *produces a tinderbox. Throws it to SARAH SMITH.*

SARAH SMITH. No, I dassent do it if Mr Coombes forbid it.

CHARLOTTE. Mr Coombes is all on a-dudder himself, he might be grateful.

They look at COOMBES. He shivers, his teeth are chattering.

KITTY. Mr Coombes, it is so rafty in here and you so still, we are concerned for your remaining extremities. Would be an awful shame for the other one to drop off, do you not agree?

SALLY *laughs.* COOMBES *glares* at KITTY *but presently, he nods.*

There you are, crack on.

SARAH SMITH. Ann, will you help me?

SARAH SMITH *and* ANN *try to get a spark from the tinderbox.*
ELIZABETH *kneels in front of* SALLY, *tries to take her hands,* SALLY *evades her.*

ELIZABETH. Sally listen to me.

SALLY. Don't.

SALLY *tries to move away but* ELIZABETH *pursues her.*

ELIZABETH. You must help the ladies to like you. You must try to appear governable, tell them what he did to you, for whatever happened, I know you did not act of your own free / will

SALLY. Are you deaf, slamkin, I said do not touch me!

SALLY *shoves her away,* ELIZABETH *falls.* COOMBES *rushes to help her up.*

ELIZABETH. That's alright. I'm alright.

ANN. There she goes.

They have produced a spark that has caught the kindling. The fire starts to take.

SARAH SMITH. Quick, the bellows.

They pump air into the fire. JUDITH *exhales and starts to fan herself.*

CHARLOTTE. Mrs Luke, you will do yourself an injury trying to find a lick of good in that girl. Why do you care so much?

ELIZABETH. Because I pulled her into the world! And I will not be part of the fury that sends her out of it!

EMMA. It is not helpful to remember people as babies when considering their deeds as grown women.

ELIZABETH. Why?

EMMA....

CHARLOTTE. It is sentimental and intellectually bankrupt.

EMMA. Yes, exactly, thank you Mrs Cary, that is what I was going / to say

CHARLOTTE. You are soft-hearted, and weak with it, Mrs Luke.

ELIZABETH. Not at all. Quite the opposite in fact, I am a hard selfish creature who dislikes having her sleep disturbed, and I do not want to lie awake tonight and wonder if I have had a hand in the unholy murder of an innocent, you are not pumping hard enough, give it here.

The fire is struggling. She grabs the bellows and pumps air vigorously into the fire.

CHARLOTTE. You do not strike me as devout. You do believe in a Heaven then?

ELIZABETH. It is impossible to look at the sky at times and not believe in it.

HELEN. The skies are very wide in this part of the country.

SARAH SMITH. Ent she got strong arms?

JUDITH. I wonder if we cracked the window, that might help to / draw the

But the fire is kicking into life now. ELIZABETH *tosses the bellows down.*

ELIZABETH. Please. This whole affair is a farce. We are cold, hungry, tired, thirsty women and all of us've had our housework interrupted. Peg does not trust the girl because she is poor while her poverty endears her to Helen, Kitty and Hannah believe she has been framed by a comet and yet will show her no mercy, Charlotte is a stranger who arrived with her mind already decided, Sarah Hollis will not speak, Ann has not slept a full night for three years, Mary, forgive me love, does not know which glove belongs on which hand,

Emma cares for nutmegs above life itself, poor Judith is dying of heat while the rest of us freeze to death and all of us are half-occupied with who is feeding the children and whether the dog has got at the cream.

It is a poor apparatus for justice. But it is what we have. This room. The sky outside that window and our own dignity beneath it. Mary's view is as important as Charlotte's, and together we must speak in one voice. It is almost impossible that we should make the right decision.

But shall we not try?

Pause.

CHARLOTTE. Mrs Luke is right. Let us pray together.

JUDITH. Oh Lord.

EMMA. A very sensible idea, Mrs Cary.

ELIZABETH. That is not / what I

SALLY. I need a piss.

HELEN. Oh dear.

ANN. Is there a bourdaloue?

SARAH SMITH. There is a bucket.

SALLY. Give it.

> SARAH SMITH *puts it beside her. During the following,* SALLY *attempts to lower herself onto the bucket unaided. It is problematic.*

CHARLOTTE. Ladies. Shall we?

> *The* WOMEN, *except for* JUDITH, ELIZABETH *and* SALLY, *kneel.*

EMMA. Mrs Brewer?

> JUDITH *is fanning herself as far away from the fire as possible.*

JUDITH. I uh, I might sit this one out. I am a little damp.

CHARLOTTE. Nonsense, you come here between Mrs Smith and myself. We are both familiar with the calamities of your age are we not, Mrs Smith?

SARAH SMITH. I don't know as I'd call it a calamity.

SALLY. 'Scuse me.

CHARLOTTE. Nonetheless, it is an alarming time.

JUDITH. I ent alarmed. I am very warm, but I ent alarmed.

JUDITH comes between CHARLOTTE *and* SARAH SMITH.

SALLY. 'Scuse me?

EMMA. Pray with us, Mrs Luke.

ELIZABETH. I will not pray with you.

SALLY. Oi!

ELIZABETH. I will not pray with you! It is not God's authority that is called upon here! You have been given a power, why are you afeard to use it?

SALLY. Can one of yous lend me a hand?

CHARLOTTE. Suit yourself. Our Father

The MATRONS, *except for* ELIZABETH, *bow their heads and close their eyes.*

MATRONS. Our Father

SALLY. 'SCUSE ME. I WANNA / TAKE A TINKLE.

CHARLOTTE. Which art in Heaven.

MATRONS. Which art in Heaven

CHARLOTTE. We pray to you in our hour of need to help us in accounting for this woman.

SALLY. Fuckssake.

SALLY finally manages to position herself on the bucket without help.

CHARLOTTE (*simultaneous with* ELIZABETH*'s line 'Account for her'*). * O dearest God, as it pleases thee, give thou message through us, to thou glory, and not for ours, or anyone else's glory, and give us a true understanding of thou Word out of thou pure grace and mercy.

MATRONS. Amen

CHARLOTTE. O God the Father, of Heaven: have mercy upon us miserable sinners.

MATRONS. O God the Father, of Heaven: have mercy upon us miserable sinners.

CHARLOTTE. Remember not, Lord, our offences, nor the offences of our forefathers. From all evil and mischief, and from everlasting damnation

MATRONS. Good Lord, deliver us.

CHARLOTTE. From all the deceits of the world, the flesh, and the Devil

MATRONS. Good Lord, deliver us.

CHARLOTTE. From lightning and tempest; from earthquake, fire, and flood; from plague, pestilence, and famine; from battle and murder, and from sudden death,

MATRONS. Good Lord, deliver us.

CHARLOTTE. From all sedition, privy conspiracy, and rebellion

MATRONS. Good Lord, deliver us.

CHARLOTTE. That it may please thee to keep all the nobility, and the Magistrates, giving them grace to execute justice, and to maintain truth

MATRONS. *We beseech thee to hear us, good Lord.*

ELIZABETH (*simultaneous with* CHARLOTTE*'s line 'O dearest God'*). * Account for her, you will not account for her! A woman is not a laundry list! Perhaps she is wicked and stupid, but so might we be, had we spent our lives suspected of of of of of broken windows and stolen nutmegs and missing stomachers, or suffered a mother, drunk every night, beaten every night, opiated every night, or a brother who came into her bed, or a father who came into her bed, or a father, a brother, an uncle, a piece of farming equipment that came into her bed, the lack of a bed wholly, the bad sleep that is taken on cold stone, the bad humour that follows, night after night, till mood becomes character, the drinking of gin through childhood, a blow to the skull, a canker, undetected or perhaps, perhaps she was, perhaps she was simply born bad but I do not think so, cos I caught her as she came out, and she was beautiful – Sally you were, a pink crumpled chitty-faced thing, so no. She was not born bad, I do not even think there is bad in her now, only an absence of good, except for the child, if you can look at a live woman and see only a dead thing, at least consider there might be a child STOP PRAYING! STOP PRETENDING TO BE CIVILISED WOMEN THIS IS NOT CIVIL

SALLY finishes with the bucket. The fire is roaring now.

SALLY. S'better.

COOMBES. Lizzy, calm / yourself

ELIZABETH. YOU ARE NOT ALLOWED TO TALK WE ARE ALLOWED TO TALK YOU ARE NOT ALLOWED TO TALK.

JUDITH suddenly breaks the circle, desperately tries to open the window.

JUDITH. I'm sorry, I cannot, I am burning, I am burning up.

CHARLOTTE. We are not finished Mrs Brewer.

SARAH SMITH rushes to help JUDITH.

JUDITH. Mrs Cary, no offence but you're driving me shanny.

The window opens. The sound of the crowd. JUDITH leans into the cool breeze. SARAH SMITH wipes JUDITH's forehead with her skirt.

SARAH SMITH. You want letting. I was let once a week, saved me that did. If we only had a knife –

EMMA. I have a knife.

She takes out a knife and offers it.

SARAH SMITH. Sit there. Get your big toe out.

JUDITH *sits down and takes her shoe off while* SARAH SMITH *collects the coal scuttle from the fireplace and the knife from* EMMA.

KITTY. Always travel armed, do you Mrs Jenkins?

EMMA. I always carry a knife. I've carried a knife since my uncle came home from the Navy when I was a girl.

KITTY. He give it to you did he?

EMMA. No.

CHARLOTTE. Mrs Jenkins, we are still praying.

EMMA. Forgive me Mrs Cary, you are quite right.

SARAH SMITH *returns to* JUDITH *with the knife and the coal scuttle.*

CHARLOTTE. O Lamb of God, that takest away the sins of the world

MATRONS. Grant us thy peace.

CHARLOTTE. O Lamb of God, that takest away the sins of the world

MATRONS. Have mercy upon us.

CHARLOTTE. O Christ, hear us.

MATRONS. O Christ, hear us.

CHARLOTTE. Lord, have mercy upon us.

MATRONS. Lord, have mercy upon us.

CHARLOTTE. Christ, have mercy upon us.

MATRONS. Christ, have mercy upon us.

SARAH SMITH. Won't take a minute.

She takes JUDITH's *foot on her lap.*

Actually, I'm worried I'm gonna cut that on the huh, Lizzy, will you?

SARAH SMITH *holds the knife out.* ELIZABETH *hesitates, then takes it.*

ELIZABETH (*to* JUDITH). Ready?

JUDITH. Just get on with it.

ELIZABETH *places her hand on* JUDITH's *forehead.*

She holds it there for a long time. JUDITH *exhales and closes her eyes.*

The prayer continues, as ELIZABETH *cuts* JUDITH's *big toe. Blood runs from it.* SARAH SMITH *catches it in the coal scuttle.* JUDITH *exhales with relief.*

JUDITH. Oh.

SARAH SMITH. Helping?

JUDITH. Oh, that is. I never even felt that, ent she something skilful?

CHARLOTTE. Lord, have mercy upon us.

MATRONS. Lord, have mercy upon us. Our Father, which art in heaven, Hallowed be thy Name. Thy kingdom come. Thy will be done in earth, as it is in heaven. Give us this day our daily bread. And forgive us our trespasses, as we forgive them that trespass against us. And lead us not into temptation, But deliver us from evil. Amen.

CHARLOTTE. Glory be to the Father, and to the Son, and to the Holy Ghost; as it was in the beginning, is now, and ever shall be, world without end. Amen.

MATRONS. Amen.

The room is still.

The sound of a baby's cry drifts through the window.

The MATRONS *and* COOMBES *all look towards the sound.*

SALLY *moves towards the window.*

Pause.

Can shut that now. That's taken the heat wholly out of me, that has.

SARAH SMITH *takes out a handkerchief, bandages* JUDITH's *toe.* ELIZABETH *shuts the window.*

A terrible flapping of wings in the chimney. Frantic. Loud. The MATRONS *look.*

CHARLOTTE. It is only the wind.

SALLY *feels a leaking sensation. Looks down in surprise.*

SALLY. Give us that glass.

ELIZABETH *looks up.*

ELIZABETH. What is it?

SALLY. Dunno. Leaking or something.

She rushes to SALLY, *hands her a glass.*
SALLY *starts trying to squeeze colostrum from herself. Still bound, it is difficult.*
The flapping gets louder. Some MATRONS *move to the fireplace, curious, unnerved.*

MARY. Is it an angel?

EMMA. Oh shut up Mary.

MARY. Put it out! Put it out!

EMMA. Don't *clutch* at me.

SALLY. Look. It is coming. I told you it would come.

She squeezes colostrum into the glass. ELIZABETH *sees, amazed.*

ELIZABETH. Let / me [help]

SALLY. Don't crowd me!

ELIZABETH. Sorry.

The flapping grows louder, more frantic.

MARY. I do not want to see an angel I am frightened to!

EMMA. Stop slarvering,[3] woman!

KITTY. Ah, leave her be, her upper storey's unfurnished.

The flapping grows louder. MARY *starts to sob in terror.*

EMMA. Crying now! Why, half the time I see you, you are
sobbing over something. Last week she was in tears because
she saw a dog with three legs –

MARY *runs round the room like a trapped bird. She bangs
on the door frantically.*

MARY. IT IS COMING! IT IS COMING! Let me out, please
let me out!

As COOMBES *wrestles* MARY *away from the door and they
tussle on the floor,* SALLY *finishes her efforts, falls back,
exhausted.*

SALLY. There you are. What did I say? What's that then? Come
on gal, don't clam up now, what is it?

ELIZABETH *takes the glass, holds it up to the light. There
is a small amount of golden colostrum in it.*

ELIZABETH. Milk.

That is milk.

*An enormous dead crow drops into the fireplace, followed by
a vast black cloud of soot. The* MATRONS *scream.*

*The black cloud billows, engulfs the room like a fog and
settles over everything.*

---

3. Talking rubbish.

The furniture, the floor, the MATRONS, SALLY, COOMBES.

The milk.

Black.

Interval.

ACT TWO

In the hours before the murder, SALLY *plays aeroplanes with* ALICE WAX.

She lies on her back, holding ALICE *aloft with her feet so the child can enjoy the sensation of flying. They are both enjoying themselves.*

6. THE SMUDGE

Moments later. ELIZABETH *still clutches the glass. The colostrum is now black with soot. As is everything and everyone else. The* MATRONS *are stunned. They cough and splutter and brush themselves down.* JUDITH *pulls the dead crow from the fireplace and holds it aloft. The fire has been smothered by it.* ELIZABETH *rocks in private prayer, not yet audible.*

ELIZABETH. * sheissavedsheissavedsheissavedsheissaved
    sheissaved.

MARY. * It is an angel! It is an angel!

KITTY. Hush Mary, it is only a crow!

JUDITH. Poor devil must've gone up there to die.

EMMA. DOES THE COURT NOT KEEP ITS CHIMNEYS
    SWEPT?

ELIZABETH. sheissavedsheissavedsheissavedsheissaved
    sheissaved

    EMMA *examines her ruined clothes.*

EMMA. Look at it! Look at it! Ruined. Sarah Smith, look at
    this bodice!

ELIZABETH (*louder*). sheissavedsheissavedsheissaved
sheissavedsheissaved

EMMA. Oh, Mrs Cary, your skirts! Allow me.

She dusts down CHARLOTTE.

CHARLOTTE. You are too kind Mrs Jenkins.

ANN. Mr Coombes, I think we must give up our endeavour, we
cannot discharge our duties in such / conditions.

ELIZABETH. What? No, look, there is milk! There is proof!
Sally it is alright. You are with child! They cannot deny
that now.

SALLY. S'what I been saying.

ELIZABETH. Let us vote again. Them as can see the proof in
this glass and believe Sally to be with quick child, raise
your hands.

She thrusts her hand in the air, expecting all to follow.

Slowly there is a show of hands from JUDITH, HELEN,
ANN, HANNAH, KITTY, MARY *and* SARAH SMITH.
ELIZABETH *looks at the others, shocked.*

But… that cannot be all. That is milk. Her maternity cannot
be in question now, you can all see it. Look. It is from her,
that's come from her, Emma, look. Mrs Hollis, that's hers,
that's proof. It is proof.

CHARLOTTE (*quietly*). It is black.

ELIZABETH. only because, no… no, that is soot, that is not –
that was gold!

*She searches through it, trying to recover the gold from
the black.*

That was, that was gold, before the, I saw it, that is only ash
from the, look… look… or taste it. Taste it, that's sweet.

She licks her fingers. She tries to offer it to PEG *and* EMMA.

If you tasted it you would not, you could not, anyway you all
saw it, did you not? You cannot deny it!

She is met with silence. PEG *looks at the floor.*

You would not deny it. You saw it, you cannot pretend you did not. Peg? I saw you look, you dassent tell me you didn't see.

PEG. I don't know what I saw. It happened so quick.

ELIZABETH. Liar!

PEG. Lizzy!

HELEN. If Lizzy says she saw something, that's good enough for me.

ANN. Well I saw it too

JUDITH. And I.

SARAH SMITH. And I.

ELIZABETH. They all of them saw it! You cannot mean to ignore the truth simply cos that's inconvenient to you, you would not do such a, such a, such a wickedness! Please! One of yous speak! One of you women SPEAK and tell me I am mistaken!

JUDITH. Don't get yourself worked up gal.

PEG. Why you got such a flea in your drawers about it?

SALLY. What is happening?

ELIZABETH. It is alright Sally. (*To the* MATRONS.) Please. Please.

Silence. A growing fear in ELIZABETH. *She thrusts the glass at* SARAH HOLLIS.

Sarah Hollis, surely you do not think me a liar? What reason have I to lie? That is evidence. That is truth, look at it! LOOK AT IT!

She thrusts the glass in CHARLOTTE's *face now.*

Mrs Cary, look at it!

CHARLOTTE *takes the glass, puts it down.*

CHARLOTTE. Open the windows.

SALLY. Right, no, what's going on?

PEG. It is freezing.

CHARLOTTE. We must let the soot out, open them.

They open the windows. The sound of the mob outside. The MATRONS *wave the soot out.* SALLY *is beginning to panic for the first time.*

SALLY. I don't understand – you asked for milk, I gave you milk – / what is?

ELIZABETH. It is alright. We / will

SALLY. That's not alright. There is proof in that glass and they won't acknowledge it, that's not alright!

Outside, the mob grows rowdier. A cheerful chant of 'Hang the bitch' bubbles up. SALLY *puts her hands over her ears, frightened.*

EMMA. There goes your gold bridge, bumkin. You're in bad bread now.

SALLY. I am telling the truth! Mrs Luke, you cannot allow / them to –

EMMA. Perhaps you will discover some civility now the gallows are groaning, slip-gibbet.

SALLY. No! I will not die for an audience! I will not be a fucking exhibit!

ELIZABETH. Listen to me, it is not over. We will petition the magistrate to stay your sentence

SALLY. He will not give it!

ELIZABETH. A month or two longer and the signs will be obvious.

SALLY. I do not have a month!

A knock at the door. COOMBES *answers it. He is handed a note. He reads it. Gives the note to* CHARLOTTE. CHARLOTTE *reads the note.*

CHARLOTTE. A Dr Willis from Halesworth has called downstairs to offer his services, should they be required.

HELEN. Well I think that's an unnecessary expense, I do.

CHARLOTTE. The court will carry the costs.

EMMA. Anyway, I heard he works admirably quick for a man paid by the hour.

SALLY. I can have a doctor? Fuckssake, why did nobody say!

ELIZABETH. We do not need a doctor to dictate to us, we are twelve grown women.

SALLY. I don't care, if that convinces them then bring him, bring him now.

EMMA. It is very unconventional but I am not opposed to it.

PEG. I must say, I do think I would be more comfortable with Dr Willis's opinion to guide us.

HANNAH. And I.

KITTY. Me too.

ELIZABETH. Why should the word of a doctor mean more to you than my own? When I brought your children into the world, you trusted me then did you not? When the curse was upon you, when your babies would not take the breast, or your milk would not come, when it was the middle of the night and you did not need anything but to lie on a warm lap and cry, when your nipples cracked and your pitchers split and your husbands could not get it up, you trusted me then! It was not Dr Willis you sought then, was it?

SALLY. You waste your time appealing to their honour, them are not honourable women. Fetch the doctor.

ELIZABETH. We do not need the doctor, I have shown you milk!

CHARLOTTE. You have shown us a glass of darkness that appeared magically while our attention was wrapped in prayer.

ELIZABETH. Magic? You cannot possibly – whatever you think of her, I am a respectable woman, why will you not believe me?

SALLY. Are you dense? You have no authority here. If they must hear the truth from someone a foot taller with a deep voice then let them.

ELIZABETH. No. I want one of you cussed mawthers to look me in the eye and tell me why you do not trust me!

Suddenly SARAH HOLLIS *coughs, prolonged. They all look at her.*

SARAH HOLLIS. I

She coughs some more. KITTY *rubs her back.*

KITTY. Alright darlin, alright.

JUDITH. You sick?

SARAH HOLLIS *shakes her head.*

SARAH HOLLIS. I

ANN. She's trying to talk.

PEG. I thought she couldn't.

EMMA. Speak up dear.

SARAH SMITH. Don't crush her.

SARAH HOLLIS *makes a croaking sound.*

KITTY. Does anyone have a sip of something for her?

JUDITH. I have a little gin.

JUDITH *takes a flask of gin from under her apron and hands it over.* COOMBES *makes a sound of protest.*

KITTY. Don't gimme that, the woman's parched! And if you whiddle on us Mr Coombes I shall whiddle on you and if I whiddle on you, you'll know about it.

KITTY *hands the gin to* SARAH HOLLIS. SARAH HOLLIS *sips. She hands the flask back. She takes* ELIZABETH'*s hand and leads her to a corner. She whispers in* ELIZABETH'*s ear, until* ELIZABETH *pulls away.*

ELIZABETH. What? No.

SARAH HOLLIS *whispers again.* ELIZABETH *looks at her in horror.*

No. No, that's not, that is not, I don't know what you're

SARAH HOLLIS *whispers again.*

No.

SARAH HOLLIS *nods.*

No!

EMMA. What is it?

SARAH HOLLIS. I would. Like

ELIZABETH. No!

SARAH HOLLIS. to speak

ELIZABETH. No!

JUDITH. Lizzy!

ELIZABETH. She's cracked, she, she dun't know what / she's

SARAH HOLLIS....is important.

ELIZABETH. It's fudge!

SARAH HOLLIS. They have to –

> ELIZABETH *flies at* SARAH HOLLIS, *tries to cover her mouth, to stop her speaking, the other* MATRONS *rush to pull her off.*

ELIZABETH. She's flamming!

> *The* MATRONS *pull* ELIZABETH *away but* ELIZABETH *throws them off.*

No, why are you doing this? What'd I ever do to you maw?

SARAH HOLLIS. I must / ...tell... them

ELIZABETH. SHUT UP. SHUT UP.

> ELIZABETH *picks up a handful of soot and tries to shove it into* SARAH HOLLIS's *mouth.* JUDITH *seizes* ELIZABETH *and barrels her across the room, pins her down.*

JUDITH. OI, THAT'S ENOUGH OF THAT! Making a noddy of yourself gal.

The other MATRONS *flock around* SARAH HOLLIS, *shocked.*

CHARLOTTE. Are you alright Mrs Hollis?

SARAH HOLLIS *splutters and spits but nods her head.*

EMMA. Here, take my handkerchief.

ELIZABETH. This is, that is a dirty wickedness, what / she is

JUDITH. Shhh. Let her speak.

SARAH HOLLIS *takes some time to gather herself. She swallows. Eventually:*

SARAH HOLLIS. When I began my labours with my son that was a hot day though late in the year and I was taken with a desire to have trees all around me and not be seen. I delivered my daughters in warm dark rooms full of women, but on this occasion I wished to be wholly private, which is something I will regret until the day I die, but that's no use shutting the gate after the pig has escaped.

I found myself

,

excuse me.

KITTY. You're alright love. Take your time.

SARAH HOLLIS *nods her thanks. A pause. She resumes.*

SARAH HOLLIS. I found myself in the woods behind Triple Plea Lane. I do not know how I got there or how long I was moaning in the loam until I spied a woman, gathering blackberries, squat in front of the brambles, her apron covered in black stains.

Her skin was pink and her hair was golden and pinned like a cottage loaf on her head with a pretty stone hanging from each ear.

It was the 20th October, well after Michaelmas and too late
to be blackberrying. This is something my mother was very
superstitious about, so I called out, even in my discomfort, to
tell her not to eat the fruit, for the Devil will have put his
hoof on it, but the woman turned and said I am the Devil.

And I saw how pretty she was, and each stone that hung
from her ears was a pearl-white tooth, and I saw the hooves
beneath her skirts, and that her chin was wet, for she wasn't
gathering blackberries after all but spitting on them to make
them sour.

I was stunned with fear but could not move, gripped as I was
by a boiling pain. She said I will help you and I cried no no
no I do not want your help but I could not stop her and after
a while I was grateful for her cool hands on my hot head and
how she held me round the waist while I braced my legs
against a tree and pushed and pushed and when the head
came out she went down on her knees and I felt her fingers
in me as she pulled gently at the boy's shoulders, till out he
came like a hull from a strawberry.

And she bent her head and tore the rope between us with her
teeth and we were cleaved apart but she put him in my arms
and he began to suck straight off and for a moment I felt a
perfect happiness.

But then I heard a grunting and a snuffling and a laughter full
of obscenity and I looked up and saw the woman, in her true
form now, transformed. Still a woman, but naked now and
bald and her dugs hung down like rotten pears, her whole
skin was a rippling canker and her breath was reasty[4] and she
was bleeding from between her legs, and left a trail of meat
behind her.

I looked down at my boy giving suck and saw her bloody
kiss on his head and suddenly I was overcome with terror.
And even though I was brimful of love I thought, I had better
kill him so I went down to the river and wrapped him in my
petticoat with some stones. But he gurgled so prettily I could
not do it. So I put my petticoat back on and took him home

---

4. Rancid.

and showed him to William and said look what I have done and he was very pleased and said he shall be called Lucas, and that is how you all come to know him by that name.

I only saw that She-Devil once again, but for twenty years I have been in terror and seen her bloody kiss on his head every day, though no one else could see it. And I lived each day fearful of what wickedness I might have delivered into the world. But I must admit Lucas has turned out a gentle boy and very Christian and cannot bear to see a bee trapped in the house but he will spend half an hour coaxing that out with a broom, I will take a little more of that gin if you could spare it, that's just the job, that is.

CHARLOTTE *hands her the gin. She drinks it off.*

HANNAH. When?

SARAH HOLLIS. What's that?

HANNAH. When d'you see that She-Devil again?

SARAH HOLLIS. Oh. Yes, so this is my point, it was in the woods the following spring, she was on her knees pulling this one out of that one.

She gestures from SALLY *to* ELIZABETH. *The* WOMEN *all look at* ELIZABETH.

ELIZABETH. Congratulations Mrs Hollis, you have wasted us ten minutes on a fairytale, perhaps we might now return to the job in hand?

SALLY. Shut up.

ELIZABETH. Sally, Mrs Hollis has not been well these / last years

SALLY. Will you cheese it one minute?

ELIZABETH. your mother, she will tell you

SALLY. My mother is not speaking to me at present.

ELIZABETH. but I thought – I heard you were very close.

SALLY. Sometimes we are close and sometimes we are at odds. It is all honey or all turd with us.

ELIZABETH. Well, you ask her

SALLY. I don't need to ask her. She's told me enough times that she bought me off you for a bullseye[5] and though she begged you many a time you would not take me back again.

'

That's stopped you talking hasn't it, thank fuck for that.

ELIZABETH. Well that is pure gammon, that.

SALLY. Is it now?

ELIZABETH. Yes that is. That is. That is, I don't like to bring this up but

SARAH SMITH. Lizzy, that'll do.

ELIZABETH. I hear Janet is a slusspot rather too fond of a drop of sky-blue / so

SARAH SMITH. I said that'll do gal!

Pause.

I wish Mrs Hollis had not chosen today to run her mouth, but here we be.

ELIZABETH. You do not think that slarver is truth, Sarah?

SARAH SMITH. I am eighty-three years old and have never left this town. I know it is.

ELIZABETH *looks at the* MATRONS. *Realises she has lost. A long pause as she battles her rage and shame. A sound of fury escapes from her. Finally, a surrender:*

ELIZABETH. Your mother never came to me, Sally.

SALLY. Liar.

ELIZABETH. I never exchanged a word with Janet Cobb, never even met her.

---

5. Five shillings.

SALLY. LIAR.

HELEN. Who was the father?

Pause.

ELIZABETH (*sotto*). oh God…

Pause.

I was working in the Wax household as a maid of all work and quartered in a garret room. I was thirteen and very ignorant. I did not know to put the chest of drawers against the door when Mr Wax and his friends came visiting from Oxford. I can't tell you who the gentlemen was as it was dark so he was more of a smell and a stubble than anything else. I went home when I started to show. I expected Mother to be on the high ropes but she said she would speak to a local woman who had recently lost a child in labour, who would be happy to take it. I was not aware payment changed hands but. Perhaps… my mother was… very careful with money.

SARAH SMITH. Susan'd lick the whitening off the wall.

ELIZABETH. I said would that not be a very wicked thing to do and she said no, because I was not to do anything. I only had to let it happen.

So I took it back to the woods and I laid it on a stump and I turned around and counted to a hundred. And whoever come, I did not even hear them, for I was staring up at the sky at a cloud shaped like a flat iron and I could hear only birdsong and the cows moaning and somewhere nearby the pounding of a butter churn.

And when I came to a hundred and turned round you were gone. So I went home. Boiled the linens.

She clears her throat. A pause.

There you are then. You all have one more wrinkle in your arse now don't you? Is there any of that gin left?

SARAH HOLLIS *gives her the flask, she drinks.*

MARY. Well ent that a caution?

HANNAH. I am fair stammed.

CHARLOTTE. You should have / declared it.

HANNAH. Wholly stammed I am, Kitty, are you –

KITTY. Aye.

JUDITH. Imagine keeping that squat from us the whole time.

ANN. I agree, you should have told us.

ELIZABETH. And have you decide I am governed by my womb and not my brain? Accuse me of feeling and not thinking, when I have come here as a rational creature, not some duzzy mawther –

HELEN. No one thinks you duzzy.

ELIZABETH. Yes. Yes they do, cos Mrs Hollis could not keep her potato trap shut!

EMMA. You lied to us!

ELIZABETH. That's got no bearing on our discussions, none / whatsoever

CHARLOTTE. You have been queering the pitch since you walked in the room!

ANN. It does put things in rather a different light.

HELEN. Lizzy, you must admit, you have a bond with the prisoner which / is

ELIZABETH. No.

HELEN. But / how

ELIZABETH. Because I do not love that thing. I never have.

,

HELEN. But there must be – you must admit some, a, a, a feeling

ELIZABETH. No.

HELEN. some tenderness / or

ELIZABETH. No.

HELEN. At the very least you must have thought of her / every day.

ELIZABETH. No. Honestly, I did not. Helen listen to me

She reaches for HELEN.

HELEN. No.

ELIZABETH. But

HELEN. Please do not touch me.

SALLY starts to laugh.

SARAH SMITH. Why you laughing gal?

SALLY. I don't know. I think I am nervous.

ELIZABETH *looks around at the* MATRONS, *who keep their distance from her.*

ELIZABETH. Please. Believe me. I did not come here in love. I come here in rage, being as I knew this building could not be decent to her. It was not built for her. It was not built for none of us. It weren't built for me, and it weren't built for Janey Nelson when her husband knocked her teeth out, or when they hanged her for catching rabbits, or when, I tell you what, tell you what, it weren't built for your old aunt, Helen, was it? When she petitioned this court for protection from her neighbours accusing her of witchcraft, did they give it?

'

Did they give it Helen?

HELEN. No.

ELIZABETH. No, and what happened?

HELEN. She was put to swim in the lake.

ELIZABETH. She was, and she nearly drowned did she not?

HELEN. Yes.

ELIZABETH. Yes, which is a horrible death but luckily for her it was the pneumonia that got her two weeks later instead, cos that Justice downstairs couldn't bring himself to keep an old woman out of a cold lake on a winter's day, and maybe you think what I done is shabby but this building is shabbier, that's a shabby useless rotten place that wants burning down, you ask me.

JUDITH. I do think we need to have that doctor in, don't you?

MARY. I do.

ANN. I have to say, I am finding this very discombobulating.

KITTY. Aye, it's a shit show.

EMMA. And Mrs Smith, I would've expected better from you. Why did you not speak up?

SARAH SMITH. I did not want her to be blamed. That child is not her fault.

CHARLOTTE. Then whose fault is she?

CHARLOTTE *has been trying to maintain her composure, a battle she gradually loses as her accent begins to slip from RP to Norfolk.*

Who are we to blame, if not you? She is a devil of your making. I don't doubt it was hard for you to cast off a child, but you have destroyed the lives of countless people Mrs Luke, how dare you boast of your dispassion! The girl has visited horror upon horror upon the world, and had Mrs Hollis not bravely spoken up she might be free to do it again, and again, / and again

EMMA. Calm yourself Mrs Cary, we will speak to the Justice.

CHARLOTTE. I do not want to speak to the Justice. I want that doctor brought in, and I want the drab hung, today.

COOMBES *moves towards the door,* ELIZABETH *blocks it.*

ELIZABETH. No.

EMMA. Really Mrs Cary, you will do yourself a / mischief

CHARLOTTE. Please stop calling me Cary, my name ent Cary, it's Tompkins, I ent a colonel's wife but a widowed housekeeper to the Bray family in Cratfield, s'nine miles from here.

SALLY (*surprised*). I know it.

CHARLOTTE. I know you know it.

SALLY.... Tompkins? It's not!

EMMA. I do not understand. Mrs Cary?

SALLY. Annie Tompkins. My God.

CHARLOTTE. Some years / ago

SALLY. What happened to the rest of you?

CHARLOTTE. Some years ago, Sally / was

SALLY. Honestly, she were pudding-bellied before and twice as wide.

CHARLOTTE. If I may be allowed to / continue

SALLY. Big as a house, how d'you do it girl?

CHARLOTTE. I HAD A TAPEWORM ALRIGHT MAY I GO ON?

,

Sally was nursery maid to a girl of six and boy of four called Albert. One day Albert caught on fire and died. Sally claimed it was an accident, but left the household shortly after.

SALLY. That was a bad business, that. Very bad business. But you must believe me, I had nothing to do with it Mrs Cary.

EMMA (*bitterly*). Tompkins.

CHARLOTTE. Later on Albert's sister told us Sally was cross the boy would not eat his carrots and had pushed him into the hearth.

SALLY. The boy was blind from German measles but would run about as if he could see! I come into the nursery, he's

fallen into the fire. I rolled him in a rug but… I dunno what
to say, that were dreadful. Really.

CHARLOTTE. That is lovely play-acting, very sincere, I am
sure Lavinia Fenton is quaking in her boots, in the meantime,
my mistress is quite mad with grief. She does not eat, does
not sleep, will not even wash herself, lies awake beside me
all night in a terror. I apologise for the deceit Mrs Jenkins,
but when we heard they had finally brought the bitch to trial,
Eliza begged me, on hands and knees she begged me to
come here and make sure the filthy piece did not slip the
gibbet as she has slipped it before.

ELIZABETH. Right, right, and you agather, tell me why what
I done is worse than what she has done?

CHARLOTTE. COS I HAVE COME TO MAKE SURE
JUSTICE IS DONE AND YOU HAVE COME TO
PERVERT IT, BRING THE DOCTOR.

ANN. Yes, I do think the doctor's counsel / would be

KITTY (*to* CHARLOTTE). Why'd you share a bed?

CHARLOTTE. What?

KITTY. Is it not a big house?

SALLY. S'fucken huge.

CHARLOTTE. I – our arrangements are none of your business.

SALLY. I have told you the truth, from soup to nuts, I have not
lied to you.

CHARLOTTE. You *have* lied! Over and over, in court you said
you knew nothing of Alice Wax's death.

SALLY. No, I said I would not *tell* nothing, it is quite different.

CHARLOTTE. To know the truth and not tell it is as wicked,
worse even!

SALLY. That was no one else's affair.

CHARLOTTE. It was Lady Wax's affair, was it not? To know
how her daughter left this world? Pieces of her body buried

in locations you will not disclose. Disgusting things we heard, vile and unimaginable horrors, a just sentence passed down and now here we sit forging an escape for her. If the doctor does find for her claim then that will be the first truth she has told us!

ELIZABETH. Mrs Cary.

EMMA. Tompkins.

ELIZABETH. I understand your fury but Sally, you must explain the influence Thomas McKay had over you

SALLY. I dunno what you're on about.

ELIZABETH. A lover is like the sun. We circle round them, don't we, if the ladies could only understand you did not have power over yourself in his, in his company –

SALLY. No power?

ELIZABETH. Exactly, that you yourself were a victim of… of his gravity.

SALLY. But I loved him.

ELIZABETH. Exactly, that is what I, you loved him, and so you were helpless / to

SALLY. No. I loved him and so I was powerful. I was not Thomas McKay's victim, I was his bride. Now I know I am short on friends in this room. But you asked for milk and I gave you milk. I have not told a single untruth to you. Mrs Cary – Tompkins – whatever the fuck your name is, I swear down I never touched that boy except to try and save him but whatever Thomas McKay did, I did also.

I did all of it. More of it, to be honest.

ANN. What do you mean by that Sally?

SALLY. I mean I do not believe Thomas McKay was real.

SARAH SMITH. Maw, there is a body lying on the hangman's table says otherwise.

KITTY. But how d'you mean, not real?

SALLY. I believe that I conjured him.

JUDITH. Now how can you believe that load of ol' squit?

EMMA. She doesn't believe it!

KITTY. She does.

SALLY. I do.

EMMA. HOW.

SALLY. Because I wished for him and he came and when he
    came he was exactly as I wished him to be.

,

ELIZABETH. How d'you mean, wished for him?

SALLY. Just that. I had been all morning mending sheets. My
    eyes were sore and my head ached but I still had the linen to
    press and the stove to black and the step to sweep, and I was
    cross cos I had only washed out my shift the night before and
    already I was muckwashed,[6] and could feel the stains coming
    at the armpits again.

JUDITH. 'Tis a bugger, doing shifts.

SARAH SMITH. Chamber lye, that's what you want to use

KITTY. Shhh, go on.

SALLY. I wondered if my husband would be in a fine mood or
    a foul one when he came home, and I hoped foul, for at least
    that means a fight, at least that means a chance to scream at
    one another which I myself find preferable to sitting in silence
    watching the wet wood smoke because you were right, there
    was a rain in the night, only you'd not hold your breath
    waiting for him to admit it and then I looked up at the sky,
    which was very blue with great round clouds, and I thought

    I thought

    I wish out of that sky would fall a man, a fine-looking man,
    on a black horse, and he would ride towards me, and stop,
    and comment on the weather, and if there might be lodgings

---

6. Sweating profusely.

nearby, but all that'd be a ruse, cos as he talked he would just be looking at me.

He would just be looking at me.

and both of us would know that all this conversing was only an excuse, so he could linger on me. So his eyes could devour me. That all he had been placed on God's green earth for was to look at me, in a way that – well that's hard to describe but I mean the sort of look that if you did it in a church you would burst into flames, that sort of look.

It would be indecent, this look.

It would put a bloom on the jam, this look.

and I wished that as he looked at me, my shawl would slip off my shoulders, and he would take off his hat and say, that's too hot a day for housework, I am going to bathe in the river, will you join me? and I would show shock, and speak of my husband and how he'd be home soon with a thrashing for the both of us, and he would smile and give me no choice, but pull me onto the back of his horse, and take me down to the wild fennel at the bottom of Nixey's field and throw me down and fuck me hard / and –

SARAH SMITH. * Sally!

EMMA. * Oh my –

KITTY/HANNAH /MARY/PEG. Shh!

SALLY. and I wanted and I wanted and I wanted and then the wanting rose up around me like milk boiling like clouds boiling and then I opened my eyes and saw a streak in the sky, a sort of dull blaze. And so I waited. And soon on the horizon I saw a smudge. And the smudge came closer and soon it became a thumbprint and the thumbprint became a smear and the smear became a hovering swarm and the swarm became a mechanical and the mechanical became a man a man a man a man who stopped before me flung his leg over his ride and before both boots had hit the ground I knew I was adrift and would do whatever he asked of me.

Pause.

KITTY. I never look up at the sky. Not unless I've washing on the line.

ANN. Yes, that must be very nice to have the time to daydream.

JUDITH. But... sorry, was there no detail at all that diverged from your... your...

EMMA. fantasy

HELEN. Hush Emma.

JUDITH. From your account?

EMMA. A vile confection.

KITTY. You imagined all that?

SALLY. Yes I did.

KITTY. And that is how he appeared?

SALLY. That is.

KITTY. And that is... what he did?

SALLY. That is.

KITTY. Exactly as you described?

SALLY. No, there was one divergence.

ANN. And what was that?

SALLY. His horse was not black, but piebald.

> COOMBES *makes a sound of disgust. The* MATRONS *look at him. He looks down.*

> The day in question I went to the house and took her from the garden about four o'clock. The earth was hazening but the day was still bright. The girl and I talked about the comet and whether dogs have dreams and when the sun started to set we played aeroplanes until Thomas came.

ANN. And then what happened?

SALLY. Thomas came.

ANN. And what did he do?

SALLY. We led her away to a quiet place.

ANN. To what end?

SALLY. To kill her.

ANN. And you knew of this plan?

SALLY. Yes.

ANN. And did you help?

SALLY. No.

ANN. But you did watch?

SALLY. Yes.

ANN. And did you try to stop him?

SALLY. No.

ANN. Did you want the girl dead?

SALLY. I don't know. I didn't mind either way.

ANN. And why did Thomas bring you along?

SALLY. Because he loved me

ANN. And?

SALLY. Because he loved me

ANN. What else?

SALLY. Because he loved me

ANN. But what purpose did you serve?

SALLY. To make her come cleanly before and tidy the mess after.

ANN. And you could not have stopped it?

SALLY. No.

ANN. You could not have stopped it?

SALLY. I could have stopped it but

ANN. But what?

SALLY. But I did not want it to stop.

A long and wretched pause.

ELIZABETH. What is aeroplanes?

Pause.

SALLY. I don't know.

There you are, Mrs Tompkins. Will you not admit now that I am truthful in all matters?

Pause.

CHARLOTTE. Bring in the doctor.

COOMBES *goes out. The* MATRONS *sit in silence.*

Mrs Jenkins, I must apologise for / presenting

EMMA. Excuse me Mrs Tompkins, I prefer to sit in silence. Perhaps if you are in need of occupation you might find a fish kettle to polish.

PEG *spits on the floor to get the ash out of her mouth.*

PEG. I cannot be rid of the taste of it.

HANNAH. I ate ashes when I was with my first. Did you eat ashes when you were quick with the boys, Kit?

KITTY. I did eat ashes and also on one occasion a piece of laundry soap.

MARY. I ate soil.

Pause. COOMBES *returns with* DR WILLIS. *A gentle man, well dressed.*

DR WILLIS. Ladies.

They all murmur a greeting. He looks around at the filthy room.

I see I cannot hope for hospital conditions here.

SARAH SMITH. We have suffered an accident with the fireplace.

DR WILLIS. Happens to the best of us. Mrs Luke. Forgive my intrusion into your domain, I am sure your judgement alone could be relied upon.

ELIZABETH. It appears you are in a minority, Dr Willis.

DR WILLIS. Yes. Well.

,

He looks to the window. We can still hear the crowd outside.

I think we'll have these shut, don't you?

COOMBES *and some of the* WOMEN *shut the windows.*

Mrs Poppy, would you hop up on the table?

SALLY *gets on the table.*

I shall do my best not to cause you any discomfort.

He takes a large metal implement from his bag. Like a speculum designed by a madman. He oils it and turns the handle on it. It squeaks.

You mustn't be afraid. This is a clean instrument entirely of my own invention. Um. Mr Coombes, if I could ask you to step outside?

COOMBES *shakes his head.*

Very well, perhaps if you would be so kind as to turn around then?

Pause. Then COOMBES *turns around.*

Very good, and is there a screen we might – ?

JUDITH. Ladies?

The MATRONS *form a screen of their bodies around the table, facing outwards, shielding* SALLY *as she is examined by* DR WILLIS.

Sounds of DR WILLIS*'s implement squeaking, and* SALLY*'s discomfort.*

DR WILLIS. Now, if you could just – that's it – a little wider. Splendid.

An awkward pause as the MATRONS *listen.*

KITTY *pulls out a handful of her hair. Shows* HANNAH.

KITTY. Told you. Look at that.

HANNAH. How long since you stopped wet-nursing?

KITTY. Not even a week. Bald by Lent I'll be.

SARAH SMITH. Go and see Lizzy, she'll give you a liquor for it.

KITTY. No offence, but if it works as well as the vinegar sponge I had off her, she can keep it.

ANN. Did it not work?

KITTY. It did not. Took the varnish off the table though.

The MATRONS *laugh. Pause. A low sound from* SALLY.

DR WILLIS. Mrs Luke, might I have a candle?

ELIZABETH. The Justice has forbid us candles.

DR WILLIS *takes a lamp and lights it with the tinderbox.*

DR WILLIS. I think we will risk his wrath. The instrument is a clever one, but lighting the dark depths is always a problem!

Pause. More discomfort from SALLY, *a new conversation begins loudly to cover it.*

SARAH SMITH. How is your toe, Mrs Brewer?

JUDITH. Yes, that's scabbed over something beautiful, that has.

SARAH SMITH. May I offer suffen else that may give relief?

JUDITH. Please.

SARAH SMITH. Bowl of rhubarb. Twice a week. Don't ask me how that works, but that does.

CHARLOTTE. Might I add a suggestion? Try not to be awake too much.

JUDITH. Right you are.

CHARLOTTE. And try not to be too angry or sad. Or excessively joyful. Do you have – (*Sotto*.) a desire to consort with men?

JUDITH *casts a glance at* DR WILLIS *and* COOMBES.

JUDITH. Matter of fact, I do.

CHARLOTTE. Don't. Even if your husband dies, there was a woman in Cratfield took up with a younger man, such a dreadful, dreadful do it were.

JUDITH. Why, what happened?

CHARLOTTE. Well, she was greatly talked about.

Pause.

EMMA. I had an aunt, fifty-two years old, her courses stopped quite suddenly, week later, she burst into flames. My uncle found her, she was two arms, two legs, and a pile of ashes. The furniture covered in grease, inside the drawers even, it dirtied the linen.

ANN. How dreadful.

EMMA. Well, it was probably the best thing for her.

HANNAH. My great-grandmother had a baby when she was seventy-three.

HELEN. No.

HANNAH (*nods*). Boy was a jibber though.

,

ANN. I do think it very queer that we know more about the movement of a comet that is thousands of miles away than the workings of a woman's body.

Pause. The squeak of the speculum in the silence.

Then DR WILLIS *comes out. Cleans and puts his apparatus away.*

ELIZABETH. Well?

DR WILLIS. Mrs Poppy are you decent?

SALLY. As I'll ever be.

DR WILLIS. You may turn around Mr Coombes, thank you.

DR WILLIS *puts the lamp down. The* MATRONS *watch him, expectant.*

EMMA. Well Dr Willis, we are all agog, what is your opinion?

DR WILLIS *wipes his hands on a handkerchief and surveys the* MATRONS.

DR WILLIS. Do you understand the difference between being quick with child and being with quick child?

ELIZABETH. Yes.

The other MATRONS *exchange looks, murmur their uncertainty.*

DR WILLIS. Quick with child is having conceived. With quick child is when the child is quickened, or moving. Do you understand the distinction I make?

The MATRONS *nod and murmur their assent.*

The prisoner is quick with child. Furthermore the child is quickened, though it is still in the early stages.

A murmur of reaction. ELIZABETH *looks down, overwhelmed with relief.*

I must depart now but I will suggest to the Justice that transportation is delayed until after the birth and that Mrs Luke is allowed to visit the prisoner daily, I suspect it will be a difficult pregnancy. (*To* SALLY.) You have struggled to carry a child before?

SALLY. How / d'you

DR WILLIS. There is an abnormality to the cervix that concerns me, and I am not certain the ovaries are without disease. (*To* ELIZABETH.) She must rest as much as possible and be fed well, with a little meat and small beer.

ELIZABETH. Thank you Dr Willis.

DR WILLIS. After the baby comes, the womb would benefit from a steam treatment to cleanse it of impurities. I don't expect the procedure is familiar to you / but

ELIZABETH. I have heard of it.

DR WILLIS. Oh, good.

ELIZABETH. I think it's a load of old shite.

,

DR WILLIS. Yes, well. It would certainly be more effective to remove the ovaries entirely.

JUDITH. Man wants to spay her.

DR WILLIS *smiles patiently.*

DR WILLIS. The ovaries are the most powerful agents in all the commotion of a lady's system. The whole animal economy of a woman makes reason and intellect a struggle. The cruelty of which Mrs Poppy is guilty does not come naturally to the female physiology. It is usually attributable to the periodic illness. If Sally was menstruating when she met this young man, then she may not be responsible for her actions. Do you have a hearty appetite?

SALLY. Right now I could eat a shoe.

DR WILLIS. Yes, I would say there is evidence for a tyranny of the ovaries.

He sighs.

Alas. The life of a woman is a history of disease. Mr Coombes.

He shakes COOMBES*'s hand.*

Mrs Luke.

He nods at her. She puts out her hand to shake. It is black with soot. He smiles, kind.

I won't, if you don't mind. Dirty hands. Bad for business. Ladies.

He bows, courteous, and goes.
They all look at SALLY. COOMBES *blows the candle out.*

PEG. Well, I suppose we must be satisfied by that.

ELIZABETH. Of course. Now you have heard it from a man you can believe it.

JUDITH. It is a good result Lizzy. Do not mar it cos your pride is hurt. Will you lead us in a vote?

ELIZABETH *shakes her head.* JUDITH *turns to* CHARLOTTE.

Mrs Cary. Tompkins. I know that is not what you hoped for but perhaps you will

CHARLOTTE *bursts into tears. Mortified, she hides herself, to recover.*

SARAH SMITH. Strike me blind, we'll be here when that comet comes round again at this rate, you agather, raise your hand if you are satisfied by the doctor's advice.

All of the MATRONS *raise their hands except* CHARLOTTE, EMMA *and* HELEN.
A pause. Then with great difficulty, CHARLOTTE *raises hers.*

HELEN *has her head bowed. She is crying.*

Helen?

HELEN. It is not fair. It is not fair.

ELIZABETH. Whassa matter maw? You were sympathetic to her from the start and now it's proven you change your mind?

HELEN. I thought she was lying to save her neck! I had sympathy for the stupid bunter. I did not imagine it could be true.

JUDITH. But is it not better this way?

HELEN. No it is not better! It is not better! She is not human, she is hell-born! Why should the Lord give that animal a bellyful when he gives me nothing, how is that fair?

ELIZABETH. It is not fair, but / Helen

HELEN. I have asked you politely Lizzy, do not touch me!

SALLY. Tell you what love, when it's born, you can have it.

    HELEN *screams in rage.*

ELIZABETH. Sally don't!

SALLY. What? Heavy baggage, innit?

HELEN. I WANT TO WATCH HER TWIST.

ELIZABETH. You don't mean that my chuck.

HELEN. YES I DO. YES I DO. I WOULD LIKE TO KICK THE STOOL AWAY MYSELF, get off me – get off me –

    HELEN *suddenly picks up the bourdaloue and throws its contents over* SALLY.

SALLY. Fuckssake. Can someone muzzle the bitch?

PEG. I know it is hard Helen, but we must find grace in the face of life's disappointments.

HELEN. OH FUCK OFF PEG!

    MARY *throws her arms around* HELEN, *wrestles her still, as* HELEN *howls.*

MARY. Shhh shhh shhh. Shhh shhh shhh.

    SALLY *allows* ELIZABETH *to dry her as* HELEN *clings to* MARY *and sobs.* MARY *sings. The song is arranged like an old folk song but is 'Running Up That Hill' by Kate Bush.*

    KITTY *and* HANNAH *join in with the chorus, followed by* JUDITH, SARAH SMITH, ANN, SARAH HOLLIS, PEG *and* EMMA.

    After a while SALLY *joins in too.*

    The song ends. A pause.

SALLY. That's a good one, that.

HELEN. You may ask me again now. I am nearly myself.

SARAH SMITH. Them as believe Sally Poppy to be with quick child, raise your hands.

Everyone except EMMA *raises their hands.*

Emma?

EMMA *stares at the floor, gives a curt nod.*

What?

EMMA. Yes.

SARAH SMITH. Yes what?

EMMA. Do not make me say it.

SARAH SMITH. You do not have to say nothing, only raise your hand.

EMMA. I will not raise my hand in defence of that woman.

SARAH SMITH. But you do believe her to be in pod?

EMMA *shrugs, mumbles.*

JUDITH. Emma Jenkins, I got a pile of ironing three-feet high a-waiting me, so you put your blusted arm in the air so we can all go home!

Pause. EMMA *puts her hand up.*

Thank you.

They all lower their hands. A moment. ELIZABETH *exhales. Exhausted.*

SARAH SMITH. Mr Coombes you may ask us for our verdict now.

COOMBES. If you are certain. You may take more / time, if –

ELIZABETH. The only words you are empowered to speak in this room by law are to ask us if we have decided our verdict, Mr Coombes.

Pause.

COOMBES. Do you have your verdict?

SARAH SMITH. Yes.

COOMBES. What is your verdict?

SARAH SMITH. Sally Poppy is with quick child.

SALLY is overwhelmed with relief. She collapses in a chair and swallows her sobs.

ELIZABETH. Well? Go and report it to the Justice.

COOMBES. The court thanks you for your service ladies. You are free to go.

EMMA. I hope we shall be compensated by the Justice for our laundry costs, this bodice was new at Christmas.

COOMBES. It is not the Justice's fault you did not abide by his rules, Mrs Jenkins.

COOMBES goes out. A moment. The MATRONS all look at each other.

JUDITH. Well.

The MATRONS rise and tidy themselves.

Reckon we better get on the road before them outside hear of it.

Outside, an angry jeer rises up, the crowd begins to boo, the sound of glass smashing.

KITTY. Too late.

They listen to the growing rage outside the window nervously.

JUDITH. You keep back from that window, Peg.

ANN. I hope it will be made clear we have only followed the advice of a medical man.

HELEN. I wonder if there is a back door we might use.

ELIZABETH (*to* SALLY). You alright?

ELIZABETH *kneels by* SALLY, *but* SALLY *does not look up.*

KITTY. She won't think herself so lucky in the end. I'd rather a flash of pain in the noose than all my long agonies abed again.

JUDITH. You were a fool to marry Mr Givens, your frame is too small for a big-headed husband.

KITTY. You cannot choose a husband by the size of his head.

JUDITH. It is as good a way as any. Will Mr Coombes return to escort us?

EMMA. I am not waiting, we've done our duty and been frozen for it.

ANN. How will you get back to Cratfield, Mrs Tompkins?

CHARLOTTE. I don't know.

I walked here but.

I cannot go home. I do not know what I will say to her.

Mrs Jenkins, I wonder whether you might take a cup of tea with me?

EMMA. No thank you.

EMMA *goes out.*

MARY. You come back and stop with me gal. I don't have no tea, but do you enjoy bread and dripping?

CHARLOTTE. I – yes, as a matter of fact I do.

Outside, the crowd suddenly falls silent.

SARAH SMITH. Why they gone quiet now?

MARY *goes to the window.*

MARY. Lady Wax just got out of a carriage. Titty totty she is.

HANNAH, SARAH SMITH, JUDITH, SARAH HOLLIS, PEG *and* HELEN *flock to see.* KITTY *hangs back, watching* SALLY.

JUDITH. Oh yes. Small as the Norfolk Dwarf, ent she?

SARAH SMITH. I knew the Norfolk Dwarf.

JUDITH. No you never.

SARAH SMITH. I did. That was in Tivetshall. Before him was famous.

PEG *sits down.*

CHARLOTTE. What was he like?

SARAH SMITH. Rather too pleased with himself, I thought.

JUDITH. That's getting dark now.

HELEN. Shutting-up time. I think I will brave it while they are tamed. Mary, are you coming?

MARY. That's not enough light to pull leeks now. Amos will be angry. Take my arm Mrs Tompkins, that's it.

CHARLOTTE. You are very kind. Please, call me Annie.

HELEN *and* MARY *go out together with* CHARLOTTE.

ANN. Did you suffer much with your deliveries Mrs Brewer?

JUDITH. Oh, no.

SARAH SMITH. You wicked liar!

JUDITH. perhaps a mite

SARAH SMITH. I heard the screams and brought the water.

JUDITH. you forget, afterwards

SARAH SMITH. Look there at my arm, the teeth marks are there still.

JUDITH. Yes. But the pain makes you love them more.

JUDITH *and* SARAH SMITH *go out together.* ANN *lingers. Almost says something.*

Then goes out.

PEG. Think I better make a dash for it too. Could someone?

HANNAH *helps* PEG *up from her seat.*

ELIZABETH. I'll visit in the morning, Peg. See how you're faring.

PEG. Yes. Yes. Yes.

,

Actually, Lizzy.

ELIZABETH *looks up.*

No I, I'll see you in the morning.

She turns to leave, but HANNAH *plucks at her.*

HANNAH. Tell her.

ELIZABETH. What is it, Peg?

Pause. PEG *squirms.*

PEG. Lizzy you been a friend to me. I do not want to see your feelings hurt.

Pause.

ELIZABETH. But?

PEG. But you know David is gardener to the Wax family and very well liked there, and. This is very difficult for me / to

ELIZABETH. Go on.

PEG. well, being aware of the, well, of, that this is my first confinement, Lord Wax has made a very generous offer of the services of his own doctor, who is an Edinburgh scholar, with no insult to you, only –

ELIZABETH. Only you wish to be attended by a man.

PEG. No – no – that is not, oh, I knew you would be raw with me – honestly Lizzy, I have been in such agonies, I dassent think what mischief it might be doing me –

ELIZABETH. Hush. S'alright. You bring that baby to me to be kissed though.

PEG. Thank you – I knew you would – thank you.

Embarrassed, she starts to leave.

ELIZABETH. Peg. Though the doctor may be expert, you have the greater authority. You know what to do. In your blood, you know. The body knows. Trust her.

PEG *nods, takes* HANNAH*'s arm.*

HANNAH. Coming Kit?

KITTY. In a minute.

KITTY *is staring at* SALLY, *transfixed by her.* PEG *and* HANNAH *go out.*

SARAH HOLLIS. I was stacking the faggots when my first came. She slipped into my hands like an eel before Lizzy even arrived, do you remember maw?

ELIZABETH *does not answer.*

Lizzy?

,

Lizzy, I know you are raw with me but. I hope we can be friends.

ELIZABETH. Do you, Mrs Hollis? I hope that for the sake of the human race, you don't speak again for another twenty years.

SARAH HOLLIS *nods, and turns to* KITTY, *who is still looking at* SALLY.

SARAH HOLLIS. Kitty? Where you gone, gal?

SARAH HOLLIS *gently pulls at* KITTY*'s arm. The spell is broken.*

KITTY. I was just thinking. It's been so nice to be out of that house all day.

SARAH HOLLIS. I know. But it is over now.

SARAH HOLLIS *and* KITTY *go out together.*

SALLY. Ta-ta then! Come again, won't you?

ELIZABETH and SALLY are alone. Outside, the sound of the crowd swells again.

ELIZABETH. They been told the hanging is cancelled.

SALLY. See, I call that very rude.

SALLY goes to the window, opens it, leans out, the crowd's rage becomes frenzied at the sight of her, a wild eruption of hatred.

Come on then! I'm free! I'm free you fuckers, I'll have your arses make buttons – ow!

She retreats and shuts the window. A stone has been thrown at her, caught her cheek, there is blood. She wipes it, looks at her fingers, laughs.

Was a child threw that. Not more than seven years old. Hard not to be impressed by that.

ELIZABETH. You are not free.

SALLY. What?

ELIZABETH. You'll live, is all. But you won't be free. You'll be transported.

SALLY. Good. I hate this country. I will go to America and have His baby and continue His work, killing any bitch who has more than I do.

ELIZABETH hides her face in horror. SALLY opens her arms, a baby voice:

Mummy!

COOMBES returns.

ELIZABETH. Mr Coombes, may I bring the prisoner some food and water?

COOMBES. Please stop pretending you have one cannikin of respect for my authority, Mrs Luke.

,

ELIZABETH. Alright then.

ELIZABETH goes out. A pause.

COOMBES. Lady Wax wishes to see you.

SALLY. What? No, I don't want to –

But COOMBES *goes out again.*

,

LADY MARIA WAX enters, followed by COOMBES. *She is very wealthy, and dressed in mourning blacks. There is a black veil covering her face.* LADY WAX *looks at* SALLY *for a long time.*

I never took them stomachers.

Another long pause.

Eventually LADY WAX *turns to* COOMBES. *She takes his hand, holds it, looks up toward the sky. He looks up too.*

She takes out a coin purse full of money. She gives it to COOMBES.

He looks at it for a long time.

Shakes his head, tries to give it back.

She refuses. Gently pushes it back towards him.

A pause.

He bows, and puts it in his pocket.

LADY WAX *exits.*

COOMBES *closes the door behind her and locks it, taking his time.*

What did the Justice say?
Do you think he will transport me?
I would like to be transported.
Don't tell him that or it might go against me, why are you *crying*?

COOMBES *knocks* SALLY *to the floor and stamps on her stomach twelve times.*

He gathers himself.
Puts her on a chair.
She clutches herself, in unthinkable pain.
Pause.
The doorknob rattles.
COOMBES *goes to the door, unlocks it.*
ELIZABETH *comes in with a tray of bread and water.*
He cannot look her in the eye.

COOMBES. She's had an accident. Clean it.

SALLY *moans.* ELIZABETH *drops the tray.*

ELIZABETH. * Oh my – what's happened? Can you stand?

SALLY. * oh no... oh no... oh no...

She tries to help SALLY *up but* SALLY *groans, falls to her hands and knees. She feels herself. Blood on her fingers.*

ELIZABETH. Oh my – fetch the doctor Billy!

COOMBES. Doctor's gone.

ELIZABETH. Well send someone after him! I don't understand, how / did this?

SALLY. Ask him.

ELIZABETH looks at COOMBES, but he avoids her eye. She understands in horror.

ELIZABETH. No. Billy, you – you dassent disrespect the authority of the court like this.

SALLY. Think Billy takes his orders from a higher authority.

ELIZABETH. Where you going, come you here!

He tries to exit. She gets between him and the door.

COOMBES. No, I must inform the Justice.

He tries to get past her, they wrestle.

ELIZABETH. Yeah? You tell him I got some information / for him too!

COOMBES. Out my way woman.

She smacks his bad arm, he cries out. She grabs him by the bollocks.

ELIZABETH. No, Lady Wax laughs at you, Billy.

And that little girl woulda grown to laugh at you too.

And one day, when you're lame, or sickening, or old, or no longer useful to them they'll untie you from your cottage and never think about you again.

SALLY groans. ELIZABETH lets COOMBES go, he goes out, in pain.

SALLY hauls herself onto a chair.

Are you… how are you?

SALLY. not too fierce

ELIZABETH. what do I… what do I… what do I, what do I do?

SALLY. leave me alone

ELIZABETH. Someone'll get a nubbing for this, I promise you.

SALLY. Think that's unlikely but – no, fuck off.

ELIZABETH has tried to put an arm around her, SALLY throws her off. Breathes through pain. ELIZABETH tries to touch her again, SALLY bats her away roughly.

You deaf or suffen? Don't want you. Enduring woman. Constant woman. Fuck your fortitude. I have done this enough times alone in the woods, I do not need you.

The pain becomes sharper, she cries out.

Would you – can you loosen these stays?

ELIZABETH loosens her stays.

ELIZABETH. Better?

SALLY nods. Pause. She breathes through her agony.

SALLY. They'll hang me now, will they?

ELIZABETH....

SALLY. Oh well. I done most things I wanted to do, except there is a pig that can spell gonna be at the fair this year but I expect that's only a midget in a costume. Are they still out there?

ELIZABETH. Only a few.

SALLY. Liar. How many?

ELIZABETH. Perhaps three hundred.

SALLY. They come for a hanging. Now they're raw they ent getting one. Ah well. They'll be twice as pleased when it happens after all.

She cries out, unable to control it.

ELIZABETH. It won't happen. It can't happen, I won't let it.

SALLY. You are like a little child sometimes, did you know that? Kill me.

ELIZABETH. What?

SALLY. Please.

ELIZABETH. Sally.

SALLY. I will not die in front of that mob. I cannot stomach it. Better in here, in the dark, in private, with dignity, could I not have a little dignity?

ELIZABETH. It is usually quick.

SALLY. The drop is not long enough. They shortened it specially, please –

ELIZABETH. I know it is frightening but you will not / feel it

SALLY. Yes but your guts go. Didn't you know that? I will die with shit running down my legs and my tongue hanging out, foaming at the mouth and women will strip my clothes like skin from a chicken so they might have something to bring out when relatives come, 'look, here is the stocking of a murderess, now what news of cousin Gerald?' – *please.* You could get a knife / or

ELIZABETH. No.

SALLY. or a brick, there must be a / piece of

ELIZABETH. Stop it

SALLY. something here, a chair, / the leg of a chair?

ELIZABETH. it is not, I will not, I cannot

SALLY. you have strong arms

ELIZABETH. not for, not for that

SALLY. or what about that poker

ELIZABETH. stop it now

SALLY. could crush my head in

ELIZABETH. Sally!

SALLY. Please.

ELIZABETH. It is not funny

SALLY. I am not joking

ELIZABETH. I am a Christian woman

SALLY. I am your daughter

ELIZABETH. don't

SALLY. what

ELIZABETH. do not blackmail me!

SALLY. I WILL BE HUMILATED. THEY WILL ABUSE ME
WITH STONES AND TURNIPS AND SHIT FROM THE
PRIVY. MY DYING BODY WILL BE AN AMUSEMENT,
THEY WILL EAT NUTS WHILE I TURN BLUE,
DANCING ROUND THE GALLOWS AS IF MY CORPSE
WERE A PLEASURE GARDEN AND THEN THEY WILL
CUT ME INTO PIECES, JOHN WAX AND HIS FRIENDS
WILL BUY TICKETS TO SEE ME NAKED ON A TABLE
WITH MY GUTS ON SHOW DO YOU WANT THIS FOR
ME? IS THAT WHAT YOU WANT? IS THIS WHAT YOU
HAD IN MIND WHEN YOU TOOK YOURSELF TO THE
WOODS TO BEAR ME? Ow

A spasm of pain. SALLY *is arrested but breathes through it.*

ELIZABETH. I am sorry – I cannot – I want to – help you but – I cannot do that.

SALLY. It is alright. I had you for one of the ones who would buckle if you shouted at them long enough. It's to your credit. Is Oliver Akas out there?

ELIZABETH. I don't know.

SALLY. Well look then.

  ELIZABETH *looks.*

ELIZABETH. I don't... oh... yes, I think I do see him.

SALLY. Alone?

ELIZABETH. No, he has brought his children.

SALLY. How many?

ELIZABETH. Three.

SALLY. Handsome.

ELIZABETH. The littlest one is jaundiced / but

SALLY. fuckssake, not the squeakers, him.

ELIZABETH. Not my type.

SALLY. he is mine. Blonde as barley and dimples like thumb marks in dough, I fucked that boy sideways for two summers, near as broke it off he said and now –

  SALLY *groans and doubles over with another spasm of pain.*

  ELIZABETH *moves towards her, attempts comfort. But* SALLY *growls and barks at her like an animal until she retreats.*

  EMMA *returns, hurried.*

EMMA. Lizzy, I quite forgot my knife, is it

  She stops, arrested by the sight of SALLY.

  What's happened?

ELIZABETH. The baby is lost.

EMMA. How? I mean… how?

ELIZABETH. I suspect Lady Wax did not like the verdict.

EMMA looks aghast at the spectacle of SALLY.

EMMA. We must – we must tell the Justice.

ELIZABETH. Tell him what? He will not believe it. And even if he does – the child is lost Emma. I will not be able to convince them otherwise, not with this… with this…

She looks at the blood spreading from SALLY.

EMMA. But

ELIZABETH. They will hang her! I, I do not know what to do… she wants… she has asked me to…

EMMA. What?

ELIZABETH. I cannot… I cannot say it.

EMMA understands. Looks at SALLY. *A pause.*

EMMA. Well. Perhaps it would be the kindest thing.

They are drunk and yowling like cats out there. I am frightened to leave by the front door. Sarah Hollis had a pig's pizzle thrown at her as she departed. There is a moral slippage in this country I find most troubling. If I were the Justice they should all of them spend the night in the cells and be whipped for breakfast. Savages.

SALLY. Emma… Emma… Emma… Emma…

EMMA. What?

SALLY. I did take those nutmegs.

EMMA. I see.

SALLY. And also a handful of cloves.

EMMA. Well –

SALLY. And a small brass bell from the counter, I don't know why. I am sorry though. Will you forgive me?

EMMA. No.

SALLY. No, fair enough. Will you tell her then?

EMMA. Tell her what?

SALLY. She's got strong arms, she could do it if she wanted.

EMMA. You know I am not the person to come to for mercy.

*The shouts of the crowd outside grow more vicious. They
scream – 'cunt bitch devil whore unrig the drab' – and clods
are hurled against the windows. It is frightening.*

SALLY *starts to cry. It is real.*

Over a long period of time, ELIZABETH *creeps closer to
her. She hesitates and retreats repeatedly but finally puts her
arms around* SALLY *and holds her.* SALLY *tenses but
allows it.*

EMMA *finds her knife and sits. Looks at them for some time.
She looks at her knife.*

We had a dog once, a brindled bitch I joked my husband
preferred to me, but really the joke was that it was true. Our
dislike was mutual, the mongrel bit me with impunity in the
knowledge that I could not bite her back. One day I found
her howling and puking having eaten the arsenic I put down
for the mice.

Straight off I thought, oh Lord, I shall be in trouble, Walter
will think I did it on purpose, and I did not put it past the
bitch not to have left a note incriminating me. But the
creature was in such pain, it was an agony to see it,
eventually I took off my stays, wrapped the laces round the
poor thing's throat and released her.

SALLY. What the fuck is she talking about?

ELIZABETH *stares at* EMMA. *A comprehension.*

ELIZABETH. But were there not consequences when Walter
came home?

EMMA. I cleaned her up and told him I had found her already
dead when I returned from the market.

ELIZABETH. Did your husband not find that hard to believe?

EMMA. Well yes but my sister was there also and swore blue it was true.

ELIZABETH. There is a great loyalty between you and your sister then?

EMMA. Yes. We were spiteful to each other as children but today we are great friends. She knows, as you do, some of the difficulties I have faced in my maternity, and that contrary to what the rest of you believe, I am quite a tender creature behind closed doors.

SALLY. Aye. Tender as a boiled owl. FUCK.

> SALLY *slithers onto the floor in pain,* EMMA *and* ELIZABETH *look at one another.*
>
> *Outside, the shouts of the crowd grow louder and more unhinged.*
>
> ELIZABETH *looks at* EMMA *and nods.* EMMA *nods. Unseen by* SALLY, EMMA *closes her eyes and puts her hands over her ears.*
>
> ELIZABETH *takes out a handkerchief. She spits on it, kneels in front of* SALLY. *Dabs at her face, cleaning it, maternal.* SALLY *recoils.*

What you doing!

ELIZABETH. It's time. Not having that mob see you with a dirty face.

> *She looks up, out the window.*

Oh. Sally, look.

SALLY. What.

ELIZABETH. Up there, see?

SALLY. WHAT.

ELIZABETH. That old comet.

> SALLY *looks. Breathes through her discomfort.* ELIZABETH *moves behind her.*

SALLY. It's come?

ELIZABETH. Yes. I'd thought that would tear the heavens but that moves quite slowly.

SALLY *peers up, searching the skies. Tuts.*

SALLY. What you on about? Nuffen there.

Unobserved, ELIZABETH *quietly pulls the laces from her stays.*

ELIZABETH. You are looking too low. Up.

SALLY *looks higher.*

Up.

SALLY *looks higher.*

Up.

SALLY *looks higher. Now her head is craned right back. Exposing her throat.*

SALLY. Oh... no, I can't... that's a bird, I / can't

ELIZABETH *wraps the ends of the laces around her hands.*

ELIZABETH. Let your eyes adjust, you been all day in a dark room. It's there, below the cloud that looks like a broom, see?

SALLY. What cloud? Where?!

ELIZABETH *affects a brightness in her voice.*

ELIZABETH. There! In the highest part of the sky. A smudge, fouling the blue.

SALLY *cranes to see.*

SALLY. Where? I honestly cannot...

ELIZABETH *begins to move the laces over* SALLY*'s head.*

oh

Sudden black.

7. THE COMET

28th July 2061.
The MATRONS *are working.*
CHARLOTTE CARY *is wrestling with a bin bag and putting a new one in.*
SARAH SMITH *is on her knees cleaning a carpet with a Dust Buster.*
HANNAH RUSTED *is carrying two heavy bags-for-life home.*
HELEN LUDLOW *is breastfeeding as she replies to emails on her phone.*
ANN LAVENDER *is using a sewing machine to make a Red Nose Day costume.*
KITTY GIVENS *is cleaning an oven.*
PEG CARTER *is folding laundry as a washing machine whirs.*
JUDITH BREWER *is ironing while she watches TV.*
SARAH HOLLIS *is cleaning a toilet.*
MARY MIDDLETON *is chopping leeks and anxiously watching a video baby monitor.*
EMMA JENKINS *is defrosting a freezer.*
ELIZABETH LUKE *is a nurse visiting a primary school, treating a child's head for nits.*

ELIZABETH *sees it first. Looks up.*

One by one the others look up too.

The COMET *is returning, passing overhead.*

They all watch it for a moment.

Then they look down again.

The WOMEN *go on with their housework.*

End.

LUCY KIRKWOOD is a playwright and screenwriter. Her plays include *Tinderbox* (Bush Theatre), a version of *Hedda Gabler* (Gate Theatre), *NSFW* (Royal Court) and *it felt empty when the heart went at first but it is alright now*, which was produced by Clean Break at the Arcola Theatre, nominated for an Evening Standard Award for Best Newcomer, and joint winner of the John Whiting Award. *Chimerica* premiered at the Almeida Theatre in 2013 and transferred to the West End, winning Best New Play at the Olivier and Evening Standard Awards, as well as the Critics' Circle and Susan Smith Blackburn Award. Recent work includes *Mosquitoes* at the National Theatre in 2017, and *The Children*, which premiered at the Royal Court in 2016, and opened on Broadway at Manhattan Theatre Club in 2017. It was the winner of the Writers' Guild Best Play Award and nominated for a Tony Award.

www.ingramcontent.com/pod-product-compliance
Lightning Source LLC
Jackson TN
JSHW021928290125
78051JS00002B/16